NONNI IN AMERICA

Authored

by

Jón Svensson

New English Translation

by

Friederika Priemer

Translation Derivative
Copyright © 2021
Chaos To Order Publishing
All rights reserved.
Isbn-13: 978-0-9907231-6-5

NONNI IN AMERICA

CHAOS TO ORDER PUBLISHING

SAN JOSE, CA

WWW.C2OP.COM

NONNI IN AMERICA

ABOUT THE TRANSLATOR

Friederika Priemer, who lives in Cologne, Germany, is not only an enthusiastic "Nonni" fan (www.home.funcity.de/nonni-fanclub-deutschland/) but also a state-certified German-English translator. For many years, she had dreamed of translating Jón Svensson's book "Nonni in Amerika" which – despite its English-sounding title – has never been translated so that the English-speaking world might have the chance to enjoy this entertaining and highly informative travelogue.

By co-incidence (or rather, divine providence?) A few years ago, Ms Priemer met John Wilhelmsson, the Chief Editor of Chaos To Order Publishing (www.c2op.com), and then, Aimee O'Connell, via mutual interests in Icelandic literature and religious history. It did not take long for her acquaintances to appreciate Jón Svensson, and the idea was born to start the translation process over the next few years. Finally, on August 19, 2021, "Nonni in America" first saw the light of day – welcomed by the happy trio, eager to share their love of "Nonni" with the rest of the English-speaking world!

NONNI IN AMERICA

CONTENTS

1. Childhood Dreams
2. A Trip to Jules Verne's House
3. My Journey Decided Upon
4. Plans and Obstacles
5. The Voice of Vienna
6. A Request by Nonni Friends
7. The "Berengaria"
8. A Good Omen at the Beginning
9. A Courtyard Encounter
10. A Reminiscence of Palermo
11. A Debate at Rue De Vaugirard
12. A Stranger in Paris
13. From Paris to London by Air
14. The Wonder of Flight
15. Over the Clouds to London
16. The Great London Mailbox
17. A Trip to the American Embassy
18. Boarding the "Berengaria"
19. Mr. Garfield, I Presume
20. A Tale of Two Ships
21. A Little Adventure in the Nursery
22. First Stop Cherbourg
23. The Little American
24. Daily Life on the "Berengaria"
25. A Charming Summer Night
26. America in Sight
27. My Little American Gives a Speech
28. First Sight of New York City

29. Entering the Megacity New York
30. Fordham University
31. First Adventures at Fordham
32. An Encounter Out of the Past
33. Thrown Into the Water
34. Lectures in Manhattan
35. A Visit to The Empire State Building
36. Fordham Versus SMU
37. Going to the Big Game
38. Conversation with an Athlete
39. Good-Bye to New York
40. New York to Chicago
41. An Adventure en Route
42. Stop Over in Chicago
43. A Canadian Acquaintance
44. Arrival in Winnipeg
45. Experiences in Winnipeg
46. Entrusting my Needs
47. In the Hands of the Agents
48. Elegantly Escaping Death
49. An Appetite for Denver
50. Land of Scenic Marvels
51. Arrival in San Francisco
52. Reception At USF
53. The Amiable Californians
54. San Francisco Municipal Hospital
55. A Lecture to the Angels
56. Departure for Japan

# NONNI IN AMERICA

PUBLISHER'S FOREWORD

The author of this book, the Reverend Jón Svensson S. J., was born on November 16, 1857 at the farmstead Möðruvellir in North Iceland and died on October 16, 1944 in Cologne, Germany. He intended this manuscript to be the last in his collection of "Nonni books" written by him and published by Verlag Herder.

This is a new translation into English of the original German title "Nonni in Amerika." It is a presentation of the great journey around the world which the then 80-year-old Svensson began in 1936. He traveled to and from London via the United States, Japan, Shanghai, Hongkong, Singapore, Aden, the Suez Canal, the Mediterranean Sea, and the Gulf of Biskaya.

This record of the first part of his journey, up to his departure from San Francisco to Japan, was completely written by Svensson, who also prepared the script for printing. However, he did not fully finish writing the second part of the travelogue, which was to describe his voyage to Japan, his one-year stay there, and the return journey to London.

In July 1942, Svensson was expelled by the National Socialist Gestapo from his peaceful residence in Valkenburg, Holland, and taken away over the border to Germany. Thanks to the help of some influential persons, his books and manuscripts were returned to him. However, the blow of his expulsion hit him so hard that he could no longer write. Thus, he only reached chapter 39 in recounting the second part of his journey, which ends with his departure from Tokyo.

In order that this valuable work should not remain unfinished, Svensson's old friend, Fr. Hermann Krose, undertook the task of completing the story of the world trip as a supplement, based on the detailed diary entries left by Svensson.

"Nonni in America" features encounters with such prominent historical figures as

Jules Verne, Thomas Cook, and James Garfield. It also features great descriptions of early air passenger flight, the great passenger steam ships, and the golden age of train travel in the United States.

Beyond the history, "Nonni in America" has much to offer to the reader of today. For in an age where the United States seems to be suffering from a certain lack of confidence, Svensson takes us back to a time when American greatness was imbued in the generosity and pride of her citizens. Be it James Garfield, the "Little American" or the many other wonderful people Nonni meets while in America, "Nonni in America" serves as a wonderful reminder of what America was and certainly still can be.

May this unique travelogue and biography, Svensson's last gift to his numerous friends and admirers, find the same warm reception given to the earlier Nonni books.

John C. Wilhelmsson

NONNI IN AMERICA

CHAPTER ONE

CHILDHOOD DREAMS

From my earliest childhood, my family and I lived on the cozy farm of Möđruvellir in Northern Iceland. Many games took place in the blooming meadows in front of the farm. In summer, on sunny days, I often made my own adventures in the tall grass, all alone. The flowers were my dearest friends. I ran from one to the other, caressing each with the enthusiasm which only a child can.

One fine summer day when I was with my flower-friends, I heard a window open at the gable end of the farmhouse. I looked up and saw my sister Bogga leaning out. She was trying to locate me in the meadow, and soon she discovered where I was.

"Nonni!" came her friendly voice. "Come in, quickly! We have something interesting to show you!"

"What is it, Bogga?" I called back.

"It is something very curious. Mother will show it to you and explain what it is."

I was now quite curious myself. As Bogga closed the window, I ran into the house as quickly as my short legs could carry me.

When I entered the sitting-room and looked at the table near the window, I beheld a strange ball, approximately as big as the head of a person. The ball was a bluish color and stood upon a small, shiny black column.

Full of amazement, I looked at that strange ball for a couple of minutes. I had no idea what it could be. I glanced at my mother – and she looked back at me and smiled.

"Dear Mother!" my words exploded at last, "What on earth is this ball?!"

"Can you not guess, Nonni?" she replied.

After pondering a moment, I said to my mother: "I think it is a toy."

"Oh no, Nonni, it's not a toy. Why don't you have a closer look?"

I dragged a chair towards the table and climbed upon it so that I could indeed have a closer look at this mysterious ball. Now, I could clearly see various drawings on the surface which looked like big stains or clouds.

What on earth could this be? Suddenly, I noticed letters, and words, too. However, at that time, it was difficult for me to understand what it said, as I had not made much progress yet at learning to read.

Finally, I said: "Dear Mother, please, come and explain to me what these signs and letters mean!"

"You must first try and find out yourself, my little Nonni. Then, I will explain it all to you."

I approached the ball even closer. I found one of the shortest words and tried to spell it. And indeed, I managed. Soon I had figured out that it said: ENGLAND. I recalled there was a country not far from us called England. Full of joy, I exclaimed: "Mother! Here it says 'England'! I have found out all by myself!" Smiling, my mother got up and came to me.

"I am pleased, Nonni", she said, "that you have begun to figure this out by yourself. Yes, you are right: here, it says 'England', indeed." She then showed me another, very small patch, not far from England, which also had a word on it.

"Can you read this word?" she asked me. I started spelling in my mind, and after a short pause I exclaimed triumphantly: "Iceland! – Here, it says 'Iceland'! Mother! What can this mean?"

"*What can this mean?*" Mother repeated, smiling. "It can only mean that Iceland lies exactly there. Do you not understand yet, my little Nonni?"

"No, I can't, dear Mother, because Iceland lies in the ocean, not on a ball! And the same is true for England. England cannot lie on a ball!" Now, my Mother laughed out loud and stroked my hair lovingly.

"Sweet innocence!" she said. "It is difficult to imagine. You are right in saying that Iceland and England are situated in the middle of the ocean.

But what if I told you that England, and Iceland and the ocean… in fact, all the oceans, and all the countries of the whole world… form a huge ball? What would you say then, my little Nonni?"

I was speechless. I did not understand my Mother at all. England, and Iceland, and all the oceans, and the whole earth… a big ball? No, that seemed impossible. Iceland was, after all, a flat country, with mountains on top. And the ocean was flat, too – you only had to open your eyes to see that. How could dear Mother say it all formed together into a ball? It was incomprehensible.

Mother noticed my perplexity and was too kind not to help me. She sat down on a chair and beckoned me over.

I ran to her, propped myself up on her knees and said: "Dear Mother, the earth is not a ball. In fact, it is completely flat. I have been at Skipalón, and also in Akureyri, and I have seen it myself!"

"My little Nonni, you are still so young, but you can trust me: the whole big earth is actually situated in the shape of a ball. And, that ball over there on the table is a true image of all the countries on earth."

Now there was nothing I could do. I had to accept the incredible, because Mother had said it seriously. But nevertheless, it remained a riddle my mind could not solve.

When Mother gave a sign, Bogga brought the globe over to us. Mother showed me the various countries and oceans: Here were the Faroe Islands, over there was Denmark, Sweden, Norway; also, England, Germany, France and Italy were there, and the great Atlantic Ocean. I had heard of all those countries already. Then, she showed me even bigger countries and oceans about which I had not heard before. Among others was an extremely large country called Russia. "There lived Russians," my Mother said. *What kind of strange people must they be!*, I thought.

Suddenly Mother rotated the globe on its axis, and all new countries and oceans came into sight! There was the Indian Ocean and the Pacific Ocean. And there were mysterious places with strange names: Africa, India, China, Japan.

Their names sound so peculiar!, I thought. Those countries were on the opposite side of the ball.

"People look different from us in these countries," said Mother. "Some have nearly black skin, others more brown, and others have tawny skin."

Dear Lord! What a marvel that must be!

"But Mother!", I exclaimed suddenly. "Those tawny and dark-skinned people are at the very bottom of the ball! How can they not fall right off?" That question was also answered and explained by Mother. However, I could not quite understand. It remained a mystery for me.

I focused my main interest on these big countries on the opposite side of the globe where people with bronze- and amber-colored skins lived: *India, Arabia, China, Japan*. The last-mentioned country was the one that left the strongest impression. It was strange. Although I was still quite young, a passionate desire awakened in my soul – or, said more correctly, a firm resolution: namely, to travel to Japan once I would be old enough.

Yes, I definitely wanted to travel to those mysterious countries … to Arabia, India, China, Japan! I had to see those countries and people, by any means necessary. Such a trip would be splendid!

I did not tell anybody about that resolution of mine, but from that day on, I kept it safely locked in the secret of my soul.

Quite often thereafter, I questioned my Mother again about those countries with their diversity of people. She told me all sorts of nice and interesting things about them. I took great care to keep everything in mind, and in the end, I knew a lot about those countries, especially India, China and Japan.

I learned that in India most people had dark complexions. I also learned that the weather over there was very warm – much warmer than in our country. Furthermore, one could find tremendously big animals there, such as huge elephants. Most inhabitants of India did not practice Christianity, but a few did. Many years prior, a famous man had traveled from Europe to

India in order to teach them about the Christian faith. His name was Francis Xavier, and he brought many people to Christianity in Japan and in other Asian countries. It is said that he also brought about miracles, such a holy man was he. I felt a great respect for him, and, as my Mother told me how he loved the Japanese people and their country, I was attracted towards them, too.

Thus, it happened that, of all the countries on the other side of the globe, Japan became my favorite, and I was absolutely determined to travel there when I grew up.

Growing up, however, seemed to me a rather slow process. Growing takes such a strangely long time.

The globe was given its own special place in the sitting-room. I approached it often and tried to find out the best way from Iceland to Japan. First, I wanted to travel by boat from Iceland over the big Atlantic Ocean to a country which was much bigger than Iceland. On its side of the globe, it did not appear to be very big, but when I compared it with Iceland, it was very large indeed. It was called "America," and one had to cross this country on the way to Japan. On the other side of America there was another ocean even bigger than the Atlantic. Its name was "Pacific," which meant "Silent Sea," and it stretched up to India, Japan and China.

Yes... again and again, I knew I had to make that trip, by any means.

Time marched on. Weeks, months, and years passed by.

I myself grew taller and taller, and there were new plans and new events which came to replace the earlier ones. My trip to Japan remained a far-off dream, but my yearning for far-away countries stayed strong in my heart. When I turned twelve years old, a great opportunity occurred in my life (which I have written about in the other "Nonni" books). It was then that I left my home country Iceland and experienced life in other countries – though much nearer to my homeland than any of the exotic places on the other side of the globe.

NONNI IN AMERICA

NONNI IN AMERICA

CHAPTER TWO

A TRIP TO JULES VERNE'S HOUSE

I left my home country at the age of twelve after being offered the opportunity to study abroad with the Jesuits. While my heart has always remained in my homeland, I was an eager student and traveler. My first voyage away from Iceland was sailing to Denmark, where I stayed for one year. In the book *"Die Stadt am Meer"* ("The City at the Sea") I have written about my adventures there. From Denmark, I traveled to Amiens in northern France, where I would begin my studies at the *École Libre de la Providence*.

While pursuing my studies in Amiens, I came across a book one day whose title aroused great excitement in me. It was *"Le Tour du Monde en 80 Jours"* ("Around the World in 80 Days") – written by the famous French author Jules Verne.

I read the book with much enthusiasm. When I finished, I was astonished to learn that Jules Verne, the author, lived right there in Amiens, the same city where I was living! I decided at once I must visit this famous man to question him about his great trip around the world. I reasoned that, as he had gone on that journey himself, he could therefore give me some good advice on my own aspirations.

I did not tell anyone of my plan, instead waiting in silence for a good opportunity. At last, it arrived. One day, when the director of my school sent me downtown to deliver a few letters, I made a little detour and soon found the house where Jules Verne lived.

I rang the bell at the entrance door and waited. Soon, I heard footsteps inside. The door was opened by a young girl, who looked at me questioningly.

"Is Monsieur Jules Verne at home?" I asked her.

"I believe that Monsieur Verne is in," she replied, looking at me searchingly.

"Would you please ask him if he could receive me? I would like to talk with him for a few minutes."

The girl answered, "In that case, I must ask you for your business card."

"Unfortunately, I don't have one", I replied, a little shyly. "I am a pupil at the *Collège de la Providence*. Pupils do not have business cards."

"I am sorry," said the young girl, "Monsieur Verne is very busy and does not receive visitors without seeing their business cards beforehand."

I pondered for a moment, then said: "I will tear out a sheet from my notebook and write my name on it."

"Fine," said the young girl, "but I recommend you also write the reason for your visit."

"I will do so."

I tore a page from my notebook and wrote the following:

Jon Svensson

Pupil at the Collège de la Providence

I would like to talk with you about your trip around the world.

I gave the young girl my self-designed business card. She asked me to enter and to wait in the hall. I obeyed, and she disappeared into the house. After a short while, she returned and said: "Kindly follow me."

I followed her up to a door that stood half open. There, she stopped and said: "Please, enter."

I entered what I assumed was Monsieur Jules Verne's study, where the man himself was seated at his desk. The girl closed the door.

Monsieur Verne got up, turned to me and waited.

I hastily made a bow and greeted him by the following words: "Good day, Sir! Will you permit me to speak with you for a few moments?"

"With pleasure, my friend," he answered. "Please, have a seat."

I sat down on a nearby chair.

Monsieur Verne looked at what I had written and said: "Your name is Jón Svensson?"

"Yes, Sir."

"That's an uncommon name."

"Oh, yes, here in France it is a rare name, but in my home country, it is quite normal."

"So, you are a foreigner?" Monsieur Verne asked, smiling.

"Yes, Sir. I am from Iceland."

"From Iceland! The country with the volcanoes! An interesting country."

"Yes, Monsieur Verne. It is a beautiful country."

"Yes, I should think so," he said, and smiled. "How can I help you?"

"I have read your book 'Le Tour du Monde en 80 Jours' and wanted to ask you how I might go on such a trip, too."

Monsieur Verne looked at me with benevolent eyes and said: "Yes, certainly! Why shouldn't you be able to go on such a journey?"

I paused while he continued smiling. Finally, he said, kindly, "Which countries would you like to visit best?"

"I would like to make the same trip as you describe in your book, and visit America, Japan, China…"

"I thought you might," said Monsieur Verne, "Traveling through America and Asia would be quite feasible. But I will give you the advice to wait a bit, my young friend. At the very least, you should finish your studies before you travel. The more you know, the more you will see! That is the most important piece of advice which I can give you now. After you have finished your studies, will you come and see me again? Then we can further discuss the matter."

I nodded. After that, Monsieur Verne got up and said very cordially: "I thank you for your visit. I will see you again after you have finished your studies." And that was the end of my visit with Monsieur Jules Verne.

I rushed back to the *Collège de la Providence*, filled with fresh enthusiasm. Unfortunately, as it happened, I was never able to make that later meeting with Monsieur Jules Verne, but his words stayed fresh in my mind for many years.

NONNI IN AMERICA

NONNI IN AMERICA

CHAPTER THREE

MY JOURNEY DECIDED UPON

My visit with the great author Jules Verne had left a great impression on me, yet it did not specifically assist me in my great travel plans. Over the years to come, I occasionally mentioned to various friends that I had ideas about travel and had met with Monsieur Verne for advice. However, I was not met with their support. Even my best friends suggested I forget all about these ideas. Such a journey was hopeless, they said, and I would do well to put it out of my mind.

However, their well-intended advice had little influence on me. I am a Norseman, and most Norsemen are driven to traverse and explore this wide world. It is in our blood! For that reason alone, I adhered to my hope, but I gradually kept the thought to myself and avoided mentioning it to others.

Time moved forward. Yes, many years passed by. I, myself got older and older and more occupied with other projects. My hope of making a world trip seemed to fade further and further away. Yet, I did not despair. I knew the proverb, "When need is greatest, help is nearest," and considered that the fulfillment of my life's dream was indeed a true need.

And then, the incredible happened: When I was just shy of my 80th year, the greatest yearning of my life was suddenly heard and answered!

How did it finally come about? It happened like this:

In 1935, I was staying at the big college in Valkenburg, in Holland. I received a visit by an important man who had just returned from a journey to Asia. That man, who was also one of my closest friends, invited me for a short walk with him through the magnificent park of the college. I accepted at once, of course.

While we were walking around the paths, he regaled me with interesting facts and adventures from his journey to the remote Asian countries. As I listened, my old wish roused deep within me, and the yearning for my own trip around the world came back to life. I exclaimed to my friend: "You must be so happy to be able to travel, and to have seen those enchanting countries in Asia!"

My friend smiled, looked at me and asked: "Perhaps you, yourself, might also like to travel to Asia?"

"Oh, yes!" I replied. "I have desired that all my life!"

"Then, is it not high time you realized your wish at last?" he asked.

"That is easier said than done," I remarked. "It has never been possible for me to find the time. I am bound by so many and various obligations that such a journey can hardly be considered."

My friend thought about it for a moment. Then he said: "If you really would like to travel around the world, it would please me to help you clear all obstacles out of the way."

His words moved me so much that I did not know what to say, for I knew that my friend, being a very influential man, was certainly able to do just that on my behalf.

I grabbed his hand and said: "I do! I do so want to make such a journey for myself! I gladly accept any help you can give me! As soon as my obligations have been cleared, I will gladly and immediately set out on my own trip around the world!"

Thus, my lifelong yearning to journey around the globe had gone from a wish to an actual plan, as easily as speaking to the right person.

However, it would still take a full year – until the summer of the year 1936 – before I could manage, with the help of my friend, to burst all fetters and to break loose.

After that, the great adventure began taking shape, at last.

NONNI IN AMERICA

CHAPTER FOUR

PLANS AND OBSTACLES

One year later, the wonderful dream of my childhood - and of my whole life - was about to become reality. You surely must understand how happy I felt!

I thought often about the many beautiful, new and unusual things I would see during this long trip ahead. I had longed for it so much when I was a child… now, in my eightieth year, it would become possible. The vast oceans and new countries – which I had never seen before – I was about to cross! I could even make acquaintance with people of new and interesting ethnic backgrounds and experience their customs and traditions! I would hear languages totally unknown to me… ah, how marvelous! Dear Lord! What a strange feeling to be thinking that I would be on the opposite side of the globe in just a few months now! In spite of my eighty years, I felt as a young child looking forward to everything that was about to happen to him.

It was good to have plenty of time for preparation. To prevent any mistakes in planning my route, a good friend of mine suggested I visit one of Thomas Cook's grand world travel bureaus to ask for his advice. And so, I did so in Vienna.

"So, you want to make a trip around the globe?", asked Mr. Cook.

"Yes, Sir. I am imagining a trip like the one made by Jules Verne, but mine should not be limited to only 80 days. You see, I want to get to know the various cities and countries along my way."

"I understand," Mr. Cook said. "That won't be a problem."

He suggested a preliminary travel plan but explained it could be changed at will, as needed.

"I advise you," continued Mr. Cook, "to start the journey in England. In Southampton, you may take one of the big English - American steamers to cross the Atlantic Ocean up to New York. From New York, you may travel through Canada and the United States of America, all the way across to California. Then, from California there are splendid Japanese steamers crossing the Pacific Ocean, arriving in Yokohama in Japan."

For the return trip, he said it would be the best to take another of the excellent Japanese steamships servicing the route between Asia and Europe. "On that journey," said Mr. Cook, "you will pass China, then India, Arabia, Africa, Egypt, Palestine and Greece. We can talk further about the details and organize them according to your needs." My mind reeled with imagery.

Mr. Cook added: "If you need any advice or help from me during the journey, you only have to write a few lines or send me a telegram. It is always my pleasure to be at your service wherever you might be."

"By the way," Mr. Cook added, "we have bureaus and branches in the capitals of most countries. You are always welcome to stop in there." He handed me a long list of all Cook offices all over the world and repeated once again that I could turn to them if ever I should need help.

Thus, the forthcoming journey seemed safer, more comfortable, and more pleasant with each passing day. Soon, every aspect had been prepared. I myself, however, was not yet completely free, as the lovers of my Nonni books had begged me to visit and give lectures across several European countries – and I had happily accepted these invitations a long time before.

For the rest of that year, I traveled and lectured across innumerable big and small cities in Europe. I spoke in big halls, in front of thousands of listeners; in colleges and schools, in front of fidgety boys and girls; and, to my great pleasure, sometimes in the open, like giving a field sermon. I was invited to use microphones and podiums, but I never warmed to that method because I needed living people and beaming faces around me when telling stories.

All was proceeding well. But then, like a bolt from the blue, something terrible happened, and I was hit by such a heavy blow that my world trip and all my plans became doubtful.

In the middle of my lecture circuit, giving daily talks in the shining capital of Austria to numerous societies, colleges, and high schools, I was stricken with a severe illness due to excessive strain, and was confined to my sickbed. Immediately, a competent doctor was called. After a thorough examination he declared my case severe, warning that I had little hope of recovery. Instead of a big trip around the globe, I would do better to face a much bigger journey - namely, the journey into the other world. Thankfully, I was not told the doctor's verdict right away. Only later would I learn of the danger I had been in.

After I lay severely ill and in constant danger of death for several weeks, I began to recover, against all odds. As I pulled away from mortal danger, I knew I had been saved, along with my world trip, too … and my great journey into eternity was postponed for the time being.

CHAPTER FIVE

THE VOICE OF VIENNA

For having been so gravely ill, I recovered remarkably quickly, and thus was able to resume my lecturing. Several lectures which I should have given in Vienna had to be canceled during my illness, but they were made up in a clever way. It happened like this:

A gentleman from the radio station in Vienna approached me and asked if I could prolong my stay by a few weeks in order to give the canceled lectures.

"I am very sorry, but that will not be possible," I replied. "People are waiting for me in various other regions. Shortly, I have to be in Riedenburg, near Bregenz, for instance. Then, immediately afterwards, in Bregenz, then in Feldkirch, and on from there. I am really very sorry that I cannot stay."

"I understand," continued the gentleman, "but I have another suggestion. Could you come to our radio station tonight and let us record a few of your lectures? We could then broadcast them to the whole of Austria, and further."

"I would be very happy to do that!" I replied. That evening, I went to the Vienna Radio Station and recorded several stories. Shortly afterwards, they were broadcast in every direction. Even after I left Vienna to continue my lecture circuit, it happened now and then that I could listen to my own stories on the radio.

I even had the following strange experience:

I had been invited to speak at Riedenburg, the well-known college and study center in Vorarlberg. I would take the train to the Riedenburg station between 10 and 11pm, and from there, walk to the college. The train arrived at the scheduled time and departed into the pitch-black after I got off. As this place was completely unknown to me, I became uneasy. The small station was completely dark and there was no one to be seen. I stood there, helpless, in the black of night. I could not see a road anywhere. I could not expect any help from Riedenburg because they did not know the exact time of my arrival. After standing and pondering what to do for about a quarter of an hour, I saw at last a tiny little light in the distance… It was the small lamp of a cyclist drawing nearer.

When he was close enough, I called to him in a loud but polite voice, asking if he could stop. He did, and I addressed him by the following words: "Excuse me, Sir, can you please tell me how I can reach Riedenburg from here?"

I had hardly spoken when a chorus of female voices arose in the darkness. We heard one person say: "Mother, that is Nonni!"

We heard the mother answer, "You are right! He must be here!" Shortly after, two shadows moved towards us in the dark.

Completely puzzled, I saw an elderly lady with her adult daughter. They came nearer into the light of the bicycle and greeted us in genuine Austrian politeness.

The Mother said: "I am so very happy to meet you, Reverend. We recognized you immediately!"

I was speechless as I eyed these two unknown figures. Finally, I said: "How can you recognize me before even seeing me? I have never been here, and I do not know anybody here…"

The elderly woman smiled and said: "We do not need to see you. We recognize you by your voice."

I protested, "But – we have never talked with each other!"

"That is true. But you have given lectures on the radio. We have heard you there, and that's how we recognized you immediately when you called out to the cyclist. Our house is quite near, but you cannot see it in the dark."

Now everything was clear to me. We talked with each other a bit longer, and by the help of these friendly people I soon found Riedenburg, where I stayed with dear friends and enjoyed my return to health.

NONNI IN AMERICA

CHAPTER SIX

A REQUEST BY NONNI FRIENDS

By the summer of 1936, I had finally finished making all my travel preparations, and the date of my departure was drawing near.

I must confess, I had not given any thought to writing a book about my adventures on my upcoming trip. After all, I was alarmingly near to my eightieth birthday, and because of my age alone, I felt I would not be fit for such a job.

But I had not taken into account the readers of the Nonni books.

Hardly had they heard of my forthcoming trip that urgent letters began reaching me from all over. Some of these letters came before my departure, and others followed me as far as the land of the rising sun.

One young reader from Italy had a very simple idea of such a trip around the world. He wrote:

"Dear Nonni!

You have to write down everything what you see. And then you have to make a book of it. I am already waiting for it."

Another reader from France wrote:

"Dear Nonni!

Have you already come back from your world trip? I am looking for your book in all shop windows. I am waiting for it. Jules Verne also went around the earth and accomplished it in the short time of eighty days."

A very bright young schoolboy from Switzerland also wrote a letter to me while I was in Japan. The address on the envelope was as follows:

"To Jón Svensson (Nonni)

who writes such beautiful books

Reykjavík Island"

I had never seen such a funny address in my life.

Apparently, that boy had also read the work of Jules Verne, and so he thought my trip would conclude in eighty days – and assumed I had already returned from Japan to Iceland. I must admire the international postal services: as the Icelandic post office did not know where I was, they sent the letter to Norway. From Norway, the letter was sent to my editor, Herder, in Freiburg im Breisgau, Germany. From there it was forwarded to Japan, where I received it at last.

Letters of that kind often reached me by the dozens. In fact, hardly a day passed by when I did not receive letters from friends in many countries, urging me to write down all my adventures and narrate them in a travel book. I wondered if behind those wishes Jules Verne was hiding! Although he died in Amiens in 1905, his books continued to live on. One of them led to the center of the earth, another one took place 20,000 leagues under the sea. These were prospects too great for me, I thought, with amusement. I hoped the boys sending me letters would not expect such adventures in my books!

Some even told me in great detail what they expected my travel book to look like:

"Dear Nonni,

When you write your next book, first of all, it should not be a scholarly book with many figures and names and which would smell of school. Neither should it report merely such things that are printed in newspapers. That would only please the politicians and professors, but not us boys and girls and the many other simple people!"

One reader, who must have seen or heard me at the many speeches, and who will now be pleased when he holds this book in his hands, wrote me the following utterly charming admonition:

"Dear Nonni,

Please describe especially the small and smallest details which you encounter during your trip because they are so pleasant. I don't know why. I only know that listening to Nonni is very pleasant and that I am at ease when I read the Nonni books. In those moments, I always think I am near him travelling with him through the world."

My friends – the young and the old – implored me the same way, time and again.

I promised to follow their wishes as best I could. Above all, I assured them solemnly that I did not intend to bore them with facts about the history and geography of those people and countries I was going to visit. One reader summarized it well in his letter by saying: "*About all that we are informed more than sufficiently at school.*" I could understand that. And therefore, I decided with pleasure to take with me in spirit all my friends from North and South, East and West into the big wide world, to let them see with their own wonder what I was about to see for myself.

CHAPTER SEVEN

THE "BERENGARIA"

As I have mentioned, I planned to travel to North America directly from Europe. That route would be the first stretch of my world trip. But I wondered how I should make that passage.

As a young boy I had made the trip from Iceland to Denmark on a tiny sailing boat. That was seventy years before, and it was a good choice back then. Had I sailed on a more conventional vessel, I would have missed many adventures which shaped my life, and I could not have told so many interesting stories – nor would there be any of the Nonni books! I would be quite sorry to have missed out on the pleasure of the adventurous journey on the sailing ship "Valdemar of Rönne" which young and old readers in many countries have enjoyed through these books. This time, however, I wanted to travel less daringly. Navigation systems have progressed enormously since I was a child! Instead of sailing on a small boat, I could now choose one of the bigger, well-equipped vessels.

The biggest of these ships ought to be found in England, I thought. So, I did some research and learned at that time the biggest ships in the world were the English "Queen Mary" and the French "Normandie." Those two giant ships were completely new and regarded everywhere as real technical wonders. I would enjoy such an opportunity to see for myself, I thought. Therefore, I contacted each shipping company, the English and the French, and asked about availability for a single passenger traveling to North America.

Immediately, the response was that both boats had been fully booked through the next five months! How strange to think of so many passengers heading to America!

What to do now? I turned the matter over in my mind, and I was greatly disappointed I could not experience either of the two splendid ships from England and France.

Behind the scenes, some of my older friends were

pleased about this setback. I learned this from the letters which I received from them. Those dear people worried about me because of my advanced age, and it seemed incomprehensible that an eighty-year-old could still feel wanderlust enough to go on a world trip all by himself. Yet they could not know what a man feels in whose veins the blood of the Norsemen runs.

In order to quell their fears, I suggested that I find a bold young man (more in line with their ideas of who might undertake such a journey) to assist me on my trip, and whose questions might give me a sense of what interested modern young people who would perhaps read of my travels. Several boys of the Herder apprenticeship family offered their companionship enthusiastically, just like young Victor who had gone with me to the 1000-year-festival of "Althing" (the Icelandic parliament) in Reykjavík in 1930, and who afterwards roamed with me across Iceland. However, their parents were not as eager to give their permission as the boys were to travel, so I ultimately set out on the trip without additional assistance. I, myself had no fear at all; I felt completely safe in God's hands. The only thing that worried me was that my superiors might hold me back out of exaggerated concern for my wellbeing!

Moving forward, I contacted another shipping company in England, and made the arrangements to start my world trip there. I ordered a ticket to New York aboard the "Berengaria" – a huge ship servicing the route between England and America, about which I knew a little bit already. The "Berengaria" had been built in 1914 in Germany. Originally, she bore the name "Imperator," and at one time was the biggest ship in the world. On that splendid ship I would thus make the first stretch of my trip, namely the route from England to New York. The ship would depart in just over three weeks' time, and thus, I would be on my way.

NONNI IN AMERICA

CHAPTER EIGHT

A GOOD OMEN AT THE BEGINNING

As I had some important business to do in Paris, as well as in London, I soon left Holland where I had been staying, traveling directly from there to Paris.

Even on the train from Holland to France, I experienced a little adventure – the first adventure of my world trip, as I considered this the earliest stage of my journey.

In my train compartment sat opposite me a very amiable gentleman with whom I engaged in conversation. I asked if by chance he was a Parisian?

"No, Sir," he said. "Though I am a Frenchman, I am not a Parisian. At the moment I am travelling through the European countries, but I live very far from here."

I felt curious but did not yet question him. He seemed to have guessed my thoughts, because he smiled and said, "Maybe you would like to know where I live."

"Certainly, yes, I would be interested," I replied.

"Have a guess, then!" he said. "But I bet," the Frenchman added with a smile, "it will not be easy for you to figure out."

My curiosity increased as I began guessing.

"You say you live far from here – probably in Switzerland or in Austria?"

"Oh no! A bit further."

"Perhaps Italy?"

"No… further still."

"Still further! Might it even be Russia?"

"Russia still is much too near."

"Even further than Russia? Then I would say in America!" I exclaimed.

Laughingly, he encouraged me: "America is also too near … Further, further … much further still…"

"You must live in India!"

"No, no, no … You have not yet gone far enough. But take heart, as you are going the right way."

I was amazed. "There is only China left!"

"Not quite!" he said. "There is still a magnificent country, one of the most wonderful countries of the world, a bit further than China."

My eyes grew wide, for now it was clear it could only be my heart's favorite and most dreamed of country.

"Now I know!", I told the friendly and humorous Frenchman, "It is Japan! You live in Japan!"

"Yes!" he smiled. "You've guessed it! I live in Japan. I am a French delegate in Tokyo."

Imagine how surprised I was to realize, at the very moment I was on my way to Japan at long last, the first unknown person with whom I struck up conversation was a citizen of that far-off, remote country!

The French gentleman noticed my reaction, and he could not quite understand my astonishment. After a moment, he said: "You seem most interested in Japan!"

"Yes, you are right, Sir. I am particularly interested in that country and its people!"

"And, how so?"

I looked at him with a smile and replied: "Ah, now it is your turn! I want you to have a guess this time!"

"Fine!", said the gentleman, laughing again. "It will be my pleasure to try."

He thought about it for a few moments. Then he looked at me and said: "Maybe you are a scholar of Japanese studies?"

"No, not really," I admitted. "But I cannot deny that I am highly interested in learning all about Japan."

Again, the witty Frenchman thought about the matter, and grinning, suggested vividly: "Now I've got it! You plan to make a trip to Japan!"

"Yes, that's right!" I answered, brightly. "You are a master in guessing!"

"And when will you begin the journey?"

"I have already begun the trip … right now, this morning!" I exclaimed. "Today is the first day of my journey!"

"Will you travel there via Russia?" my companion asked.

"No," I answered, "I shall travel across the great oceans, because I love to go by boat. I am on my way to London, via Paris, and then from England will cross the Atlantic Ocean to America. Then, after traversing America, I will cross the Pacific Ocean to Japan. On arrival, I shall go to Tokyo where I shall remain for a long stay."

"I am very pleased to hear that!" he said. "Where shall you stay in Tokyo?"

"In the Catholic University Jochi Daigaku."

"I know that university very well!", exclaimed my friendly travel companion. "The address there is Kojimachi Kioicho. I live in Tokyo myself, not far from the University Jochi Daigaku. I belong to a French mission there." He gave me the complete address and asked me to visit him by all means as soon as I settled in Tokyo.

We talked much about our plans in Japan for quite some time, and finally said goodbye when the train stopped at the big railway station in Paris. I would be staying in Paris for one week to fulfill lecture engagements I had booked there.

I regarded this encounter with the French gentleman as a good omen. The more I thought about it, the more I found it curious that the first person I should meet at the beginning of my journey should be a citizen of that country and that city where I was about to visit! I determined to keep my promise and visit my new French acquaintance once I arrived in Tokyo (and, in fact, I did visit him several times when I was there, and every time, he received me in the friendliest way).

I congratulated myself for having met such a cheerful new fried on the train to Paris, on the very first day of my journey around the world.

NONNI IN AMERICA

CHAPTER NINE

A COURTYARD ENCOUNTER

I had stopped in Paris to give a couple of lectures. One of these was to be given on the day of my arrival, in a lecture hall in Rue Lafayette. I arrived at the hall in the afternoon about half an hour before the lecture was to begin.

Beside the venue was a huge courtyard where some Parisian schoolboys were playing. I entered the courtyard and watched the games and the cheerful bustle. Soon some of the boys approached me and greeted me politely.

I returned their greeting, cordially asking them how they were and what they were doing.

"We have come here in order to listen to a lecture in the hall over there."

Without telling them who I was, I asked the boys: "When will the lecture begin?"

"Not for half an hour yet," they replied, "so we are playing in the open until the lecture begins, instead of waiting inside." None of them had any idea that I was the lecturer.

For fun, I continued: "Do you know who is giving this lecture?"

First the boys looked at each other. Then one of the older ones replied:

"It is Nonni, who wrote *'Récits Islandais'*."

"And who is this Nonni?" I asked.

"He is an Icelandic boy."

"A boy! Is a boy able to give such a speech?"

Again, the boys looked at each other. Apparently, they did not know how to answer that question. Then one of the older boys said: "He should be able to do that, for he has written that book himself and his name was printed on the flyers which were distributed today."

I had fun with this innocent "Quid pro quo," as the Frenchmen call such a muddled confusion.

"How old must this Nonni be?" I continued.

"He might be a little over 12 years," they replied.

The matter was getting more complicated all the time. I thought it might be time to introduce myself to those dear boys, and so I said: "Don't you think that that Nonni might have grown a bit older since writing his book?"

The children protested: "No, no! He is only 12 years old. It says so in the book and we have read it."

From nearby, a bell began ringing. I looked at my watch and saw I should go inside. I said goodbye to the children and entered the lecture hall in order to prepare my speech.

A good hour after the lecture was finished, I fell again in the hands of my little friends, this time on the main street in front of the lecture hall. Recognizing me immediately, they called to each other: "Come here quickly! Nonni is here again!"

In an instant I was encircled by the same boys, and also by many others who had joined them. I managed to lead the crowd into a small alley way, where the cheerful little Parisians gathered around me again, now raining questions and shouts of all kinds.

"You are Nonni yourself! We recognized you immediately, especially when you began your speech on the stage!"

I wanted to say something, but it was impossible; everybody was talking and shouting at the same time.

Finally, I managed to calm the small, frenetic flock by gestures. And when I was able to speak I said: "Children, what am I going to do? Earlier you told me that Nonni was a little boy of 12 years. Now I doubt myself who I am after all! I am eighty years old, after all, yet Nonni is supposed to be twelve? What might that mean, and how can we understand it?"

Now the boys almost lost their faith in me. The little ones stood there puzzled and did not know what to say.

Then, all of the sudden, one of the older boys untied the difficult knot.

He said: "I know! Nonni experienced the whole story of *'Récits Islandais'* much earlier. Then, he grew up and became as he is now."

The truth at last dawned upon them, both the younger and the older boys, and soon everybody understood that the Nonni in *'Récits islandais'* was the same but was much younger at the time of the story than the present Nonni before them.

NONNI IN AMERICA

CHAPTER TEN

A REMINISCENCE OF PALERMO

A few years before, in Italy, I had a similar adventure as to the one in Paris. While touring the Italian wonderland, I found myself one day in the capital of Sicily, beautiful Palermo, where I stayed a few days with some friends in a very fine college in the town center. On the second day, the director of that institution came to my room and said: "Downstairs, in the consultation room, there is a visitor who would like to see you."

"And who is this?" I asked.

"It is a twelve-year old boy from town. He, his parents and siblings have read your books, and they would like very much to see 'Nonni'."

I accompanied the director downstairs, and he guided me through a hallway leading to the door of the parlor. He advised me to knock when ready and left me there. I approached the door and knocked. A boy's voice invited me to enter, so I opened the door and stepped in. The young visitor was seated in a chair next to the table. I greeted him. He stood, returned my greeting politely, then sat down again, acting as if he wanted nothing to do with me. I was rather surprised at his indifference!

Without saying a word, I moved a chair towards him and sat down. The boy remained silent, still behaving as if I was not even there. After a few moments, I spoke to him in a warm and friendly tone in French:

"Little friend, I was told that you had asked for me, and that you wanted to talk with me."

The boy looked puzzled and answered, "Sir, there must be a misunderstanding. I have asked for 'Nonni,' and only with him did I want to speak."

I began to smile because I could see his peculiar misunderstanding. I leaned closer and asked him,

"Who is this Nonni, whom you hope to see?"

"He is the boy from Iceland who wrote the book about *"Nonni and Manni."* I have heard that he has come to Palermo, and that he is lodging here in the college."

"Yes," I said, "I have heard that too, and I know

that it is true: Nonni has really come to Palermo, and he is staying in this house. Do you want to see him?"

"Yes, Sir, very much indeed!" was the boy's reply.

"If you could see him," I asked, "do you think you would be able to recognize him easily?"

"Oh yes," he answered. "I have seen his picture in the book *Nonni and Manni!*"

Apparently, the boy thought that Nonni had written the Italian translation of this book recently, and that Nonni was still a boy of twelve years himself. I had to free him from that erroneous opinion.

I asked him the following question:

"When did the story of *'Nonni and Manni'* happen?"

"I don't know exactly," replied the little Italian, "but I believe it happened a short time ago."

"In that case, Nonni would still be a small boy."

"Yes, Sir."

Now I said: "If I told you that the story of *Nonni and Manni* happened more than fifty years ago, what would you say?"

The boy's eyes grew big. He reflected a few moments. Then he said: "But, Sir, it was published just this year, and Nonni's picture is in it. And in that picture, he looks like a boy!"

"Little friend", I replied, "the Italian book *Nonni and Manni* is a translation of a story which Nonni wrote many years ago. A much older Nonni is here in this house, and you have even seen him already – and talked to him, too."

The little boy was amazed. He did not know if he should laugh or weep! For a moment he looked at me with wide open eyes. Finally, he asked: "Where is Nonni now?"

I smiled at the little Italian boy and said, slowly, pronouncing each word clearly: "He is here, right now … in this room … and he is sitting next to you, on a chair. Indeed, my dear little friend … this old man talking with you is Nonni himself."

Upon that revelation, my little friend sat speechless and totally overwhelmed!

It was not difficult for me to empathize with his thinking. I, the real (and old) Nonni, still imagined I looked like the young Nonni whom the little boy had enclosed in his heart, whose boyish photograph he had stored in his mind. Soon, however, the good little boy recovered from his tremendous surprise, and soon, we were engaged in an informal and warm conversation.

Finally, he said: "As I have found and recognized you after all, you have to promise me to visit my *famiglia*, because both *"mamma mia"* and *"sorella mia"* have read the story of *Nonni and Manni* and both would be very pleased to meet Nonni themselves!"

Gladly I promised to visit "Mamma" and "Sorella."

Then, after chatting together for a little while yet, we parted as good friends.

CHAPTER 11

A DEBATE AT
RUE DE VAUGIRARD

My days in Paris would end soon. The next stretch would take me from Paris to London. There are, however, many ways to get from one city to the other. I wished to find an interesting way; if possible, a rather uncommon way, for I enjoy treading unbeaten tracks.

My accommodation in Paris was in Rue de Vaugirard next to Place de la Convention. There I made many good and dear friends. It was a big college and an important boarding school where many bright and cheerful students – both boys and girls – were educated and instructed. Now and then, I gave speeches to the young students of that institution and told them many fascinating things. Prior to my departure, having just told the students some stories, I remained with them for a while yet to chat with them about my upcoming world trip. We were seated in a nice, spacious hall. In the midst of our conversation, I asked the youngsters what might be the best and easiest way to get from Paris to London?

They thought about it for a few moments. Then one of the boys made the following suggestion:

"Take the train from Paris to Calais. From Calais, cross the channel by boat to England, then take the train to London."

"And, how long will such a trip take?" I asked.

"It takes about one day," said the boy.

"Is there any shorter way so that one could make that trip a bit more quickly?" I asked the children.

Another boy replied: "Sure, you can cover the distance from Paris to London much more quickly and easily!"

"How?" I asked.

"By air travel!" Shouted all the children at once.

"How would I do that?" I continued.

One of the elder boys who seemed to be very up-to-date said: "You take a car from here to the center of Paris. There, you get off at Rue des Italiens. Then, you get on a bus which takes you to the Parisian airport, Le Bourget. From Le Bourget, airplanes fly to and from London many times a day."

"That sounds right for me," I said. "How long does that trip from Paris to London take, by air?" "About two hours." The boy who gave that information seemed to be very well informed. But now another student held up his hand and said:

"Although the travel through the air is nice, short and interesting, it must be more expensive than the journey across land and water."

"It only looks like it," continued the first boy, "But in reality, it is not more costly."

Everybody was quiet in the hall as they waited for his explanation. I was fascinated too, for it seemed to me that those Parisian students presented their views with unusual cleverness and that they knew how to defend them. One got up and addressed his question to the one who had spoken last: "Can you prove what you said before, that the travel from here to London through the air is not more expensive than traveling by train and boat?" "Yes, I can," replied the young opponent quickly.

"When you make that trip the usual way, by train and boat, the tickets do cost less than the ticket for air travel, but there are several other costs involved, such as paying for at least two meals along the way. Besides, it takes the whole day, and lost time also counts. By plane, you only have to pay for the ticket. You only lose about two hours and you do not have to buy any meals."

"If that is the case," I said, "I prefer to travel by air."

Now one of the younger ones asked to speak. He got up and said: "It is true, that traveling by air is much faster and, in the end, also cheaper than the other way, but one must not forget that there is a big drawback: it is dangerous, very dangerous; indeed, much more dangerous than the normal travel over land. It is much safer to remain on the ground, even if it is slower and maybe a bit more expensive, than to climb up to the clouds and risk one's life."

At first, the boys did not know how they might reply to those objections. There was a pause, and then one of the older boys got up and said: "My father, who is employed in aviation, has told me that travelling by airplane was only dangerous at the beginning. Now, however, that is no longer the case. He says it has been proven that air travel is a less dangerous journey than trains and boats."

Herewith, our consultations were closed. I had made up my mind to take a plane from Paris to London.

That was the close of the short "parliamentary session" at the college in Rue de Vaugirard.

CHAPTER 12

A STRANGER IN PARIS

That I might not lose any time, and to arrange my air trip to London safely, I decided to go to Rue des Italiens that very day so that I could find out in greater detail about travel options between Paris and London. As I set to undertake that task, I had yet another strange and mysterious experience.

When I left the house in Rue de Vaugirard, I walked out to the street, looking to hail an available driver. There were none. And then, an elegant looking gentleman in a nice little car drove up, greeted me and said: "Sir, you are looking for a car, but there are none to be seen. Perhaps I could be of service to you?"

"You are very kind, Sir!" I replied, "I would certainly be grateful if you could help me."

"Where do you want to go?", asked the gentleman.

"To Rue des Italiens."

"I have to go exactly in that direction myself," he said. "Please, get in!"

Immediately, I accepted his offer and went to sit in the back seat, but the gentleman asked me to sit next to him in the front. During the ride we continued chatting.

"You are a foreigner, I'm guessing?" asked the gentleman.

"Yes, Sir, I am from Iceland."

"From Iceland? Now, that is interesting! You are the second Icelander whom I know!"

Now it was me who wanted to know more! I asked him: "Is this Icelander you mention also here in Paris?"

"I have to confess," he replied, "that I do not know him personally, and so I do not know where he is now. I have only read a few of his books. He is a writer, you know."

In that instant my amusement increased greatly.

"Do you happen to know his name?" I asked eagerly.

"Certainly! His name is Jón Svensson, but he calls himself "Nonni," as he says this was his name as a boy."

I paused in embarrassment because I did not know how to answer. Meanwhile, the gentleman continued, "I am sure you know of him, because he is your fellow countryman."

"Yes, I know him, even quite well!" I said. "Where might he be now?"

"As I said before, I don't know. I only know that he has been here in Paris many times. He often gives speeches here and in the surrounding areas."

I paused again. The gentleman went on looking at me and inquired: "May I ask for your own honorable name?"

"You know my name already," I replied. "I have the same name as the Icelander of whom you have spoken."

The driver looked puzzled, and I quickly clarified: "Jón Svensson is my proper name, and Nonni was my name as a boy."

The gentleman was speechless! Finally, he said: "Isn't this strange? When I invited you to get into my car, I did not know myself why I did. Ordinarily, I would not do such a thing. But when I first stopped, it felt as though you were one of my acquaintances, not a stranger… perhaps even one of my close friends. I don't know how to explain it." After a pause, he added: "Something unknown, mysterious, led me to stop my car and invite you for a ride."

These words of this highly educated gentleman left a mysterious impression on me. For strange and inexplicable reasons, it also seemed to me as if this completely unknown gentleman was an old acquaintance of mine, not someone I'd just met… yet we were each completely unknown to the other.

When we reached Rue des Italiens, we both got out and went to the air travel offices. Without asking, the kind gentleman helped me set up my air trip from Paris to London in the best way possible. When that was finished, he insisted on driving me back personally to my lodgings in Rue de Vaugirard.

NONNI IN AMERICA

NONNI IN AMERICA

CHAPTER 13

FROM PARIS TO LONDON BY AIR

Everything was in place for my air trip from France to England. I had only one night left in Paris.

The next day, early in the afternoon, I left my friends in Rue de Vaugirard and, with suitcases in hand, I went by car to Rue des Italiens. On arrival there, I ordered my ticket. After I had been weighed together with my suitcases, which is the custom when travelling by air, I asked when we would depart for the airport Le Bourget. One of the officials looked at his watch and said: "The bus which takes you to the airport will come in half an hour. It will stop in front of the exit door, so that's where you should be ready to board." Therefore, I stayed where I was, waiting on the bench in the big office.

Hardly five minutes later, a lady came in with her son of about 12 years and bought a ticket for the little boy. Judging by her language, she had to be English. When she had the ticket, she and her son took a seat on the bench not far from me. They talked to each other in a low voice for a few minutes, and then the lady got up and approached me. I understood immediately that she wanted to tell me something, and I stood to greet her. She returned my greeting and said: "Sir, aren't you the author of the *Nonni* books?"

"Yes, madam," I said, giving her my business card.

"I have a picture of you, and recognized you immediately!" continued the lady. "Are you going to London?"

"Yes, madam" I replied.

"May I ask of you a favor, Sir?"

"With pleasure," I answered. "I shall be at your service, however possible."

"I am very much obliged," she said. "It concerns my little boy, who is traveling to London all by himself. He is sensible enough to make that short trip by plane alone. However, I would be more at ease if I knew an adult would look after him."

NONNI IN AMERICA

I assured her it would be my pleasure to look after him and take care of him until he arrived safely in London.

"Thank you for your kindness!" she said. "There will be someone to meet him at the airport in London."

"Everything is in order then, madam," I responded. "You can rely on me! I will not leave him until he is met by your friends in London."

The English lady did not know how to thank me. She introduced the little boy to me as James. I do not remember his surname; if I am not mistaken, it was Appleton, or something like that.

Little James was very polite. I stretched out my hand and greeted him in French. He answered me politely in his mother tongue and said he was pleased to make the trip with me. Thus, we got acquainted in a short time, and it seemed everything was arranged perfectly.

"Now, Mother," he said in his native tongue, "all is settled." He suggested that she did not need to accompany him to the airport. He was in good hands and was able to cover that stretch with me without any danger.

"Fine, then, dear James. I shall go home now and leave you in the hands of your new friend." Not long after that, the bus arrived which would take the passengers to Le Bourget, the airport of Paris.

Little James said good-bye to his mother and got on the bus with me. "I wish both of you a happy journey!" said the lady, and the bus took off. The big, elegant coach rolled through the streets of Paris towards Le Bourget.

Right from the beginning, the friendly young English lad proved to be a vivacious and pleasant companion who showed interest in everything. Although he understood me quite well when I spoke French, he preferred to express himself in English.

He asked me once on the bus: "Sir, is it not a bother for you to have to look after such a boy during the journey? I should think that you would have preferred to make that short trip to London free of any obligation."

"My dear little friend," I answered, "what are you saying? On the contrary, it is a pleasure for me to be accompanied by such an amicable little companion. You must not think that you are disturbing or bothering me."

"I am glad," said the boy. "Then I am at ease. I only thought it might be uncomfortable for you not to enjoy the peace of traveling alone."

The ride from Rue des Italiens to the airport takes more than half an hour. Thus, we had time to chat about various topics while rolling over the streets and boulevards of Paris. My new travel companion left on me the best possible impression. Although I had promised to lend a helping hand to him, I began to feel that I benefitted more from him than I could give in return, as he was such a practical and reasonable boy.

CHAPTER 14

THE WONDER OF FLIGHT

When we reached the famous airport Le Bourget, we got off the bus with our luggage and headed towards the plane. It bore a nice name: "Golden Ray" in English, or in French, "*Rayon d' Or.*" It waited motionless, ready for take-off, out there on the runway. There were steps leading up to the entrance door of the plane. I asked my little travel companion to climb up before me, then I followed him.

Upstairs, we entered a narrow aisle. On both sides there were small, but very beautifully furnished cabins, each with a narrow table made of brilliantly polished red-brown mahogany wood, and armchairs with heavy, dark red velvet cushions. Though the cabins were narrow, they were quite comfortable. There were windows in the outer wall of the airplane so that passengers could have a look outside from their seats. We had a surprisingly wide view of what would be below us, which the passengers probably appreciated most.

We took our seats and waited for the take-off with the greatest excitement. It did not take long. First, the tremendous giant bird began to tremble … then, the trembling changed into a heavy jolting …and the huge propellers on the left and on the right began rotating faster and faster. The humming and trembling became so powerful that no conversation was possible anymore. If you wanted to tell your neighbor something, you had to shout with all your might. There came a moment when the noise and movement grew into a deafening rumble, a roar unparalleled, and the trembling of the whole plane became almost spooky. With a heavy jolt, the giant bird rumbled over the ground. Such intense jolts and jars followed each other so quickly that you had to grip tightly onto your seat. At last, the giant bird began to detach itself from the earth, though once or twice it bumped against the ground before it managed to finally raise itself into the air.

Once airborne, all jolts and jars stopped, for now we were flying freely in the clear. The proper flight had begun.

Looking through the window we could see how quickly we moved forward and gained altitude. The earth grew more distant, the mountains became smaller and the valleys narrower. We changed from terrestrials to inhabitants of the air. The immeasurable ether was our element now ... we were swimming there like fish in the water.

Everything on the earth below us grew tinier and less important from second to second. Even the vast sea of houses of Paris faded from our view by and by, until all the beautiful palaces and huge buildings of that megacity looked like a big box of bricks. The French capital disappeared into the distance. As quick as lightning we were flying high above France.

The air travel was now in full swing.

There was silence around us. No more jolts, no harsh sounds anymore – only a regular heavy humming, so strong and loud that you could not hear your own voice – even if we spoke with all our might. Conversation was impossible!

We looked down to the earth to see all of France below us. We could see open, flat land, and vast, fertile plains, and the large woods. We also saw rivers, towns, and big and small villages. But it was totally different from what we had imagined. The flat land, i.e., the fertile plains of France, looked as if they had been cut into small oval or square areas, even though these were in actuality huge farming fields. The large and impressive woods seen from that height were only small groups of trees. Canals and rivers appeared like thin silver lines. Everywhere were also tiny little strokes and lines stretched like strings and ribbons from one point to the other. Those were the broad ways, the country roads and rural roads of Northern France! We could hardly discern people, horses, cars; they looked like little dark dots.

We sat looking at the strange panorama below us. A steward in airline uniform appeared from time to time with a menu offering refreshments. We ordered a cup of milk for each of us and enjoyed that small treat while racing through the air at breakneck speed.

Suddenly, something new and surprising happened. Up to then, we had been bathed in bright sunshine and warmth. Abruptly, it became cooler and less bright.

I stretched towards the small window, examined the sky around us and discovered at some distance in front of us something rather peculiar. It looked like a tremendously big, dark, almost black wall! That mysterious wall stretched unto the earth below. But it also stretched to the sky high above us. It even extended enormously to the left and to the right.

I shouted to the little English boy. "James, what is this peculiar wall?"

James got nearer to the window, looked at the strange phenomenon, and said: "It's rain, storm and bad weather, and nothing else, Sir."

The English boy was more accustomed to travel by air than me.

As we reached the dark wall, within a few seconds, it felt like a dark power gripped us, pulled us from the warmth and sunshine, and flung us into a world of night, storm, and rain. The airplane, which had been floating calmly through the mild air, was now seized and shaken by the storm so violently that it began to slope dramatically, first to the left, then to the right, to that extent that we lost our balance in the cabin. We had to grip the table in order not to topple over. In fact, the storm grew so heavy that the pilots of our airplane did not dare to penetrate further on this course. They turned back in a wide arc to leave the dangerous thundercloud as quickly as possible. It did not take long, and our flying machine shot out of the cloudburst to rejoin our path in the quiet, sunny and warm air as before.

We marveled at that maneuver which had freed us from the treacherous cloud of thunderstorms. Although we made a great detour around the storm, in exchange we received golden sunshine and warm air, and thus could enjoy our journey in the most beautiful summery weather until the end.

I would have loved to chat with my little travel companion during our adventurous flight, but battling with the storm was difficult for the engines, which were moaning so loudly that we could communicate only with signs. After it had become calmer again, we looked out of the window to contemplate once more the countryside of Northern France. But – to our surprise, the French countryside had disappeared completely! We could not see any land anymore, but instead, only the green-bluish surface of the sea. We were flying over the Channel which the French call "*La Manche.*" In the magnificent sunshine, the surface glistened like gold and silver. Numerous steamships, big and small, crossed the Channel below. Watching that game below took our attention from the changes happening around us up here.

NONNI IN AMERICA

CHAPTER 15

OVER THE CLOUDS TO LONDON

After the storm's throwing us to and fro, along with the deafening noise of the propellers working at full speed, the quiet that followed almost seemed sinister. But soon, were glad we could hear one another without having to shout and brace as before.

"Now, we shall reach England soon," James announced.

Indeed, we lost sight of the French coast. In exchange, England would be soon in front of us, but we could not see it yet. James was sitting opposite me looking out of the window. After the wild rocking game in the black cloud, I wondered how he could seem so composed. For that reason, I inquired: "How are you James?"

"Very well, Sir," he called back cheerfully.

"Did you not become even a bit airsick when we were in that storm cloud?" I asked him, probing a bit deeper.

"Oh, no! In fact, I have never been airsick or seasick!" was his clear and convincing answer.

"I am glad to hear that," I said. "I cannot say the same about myself; I have often been seasick."

James had been looking through the window with increasing frequency. Although the little Englishman showed great control of his feelings, he did not want to miss the moment when his homeland came into sight. But then, something completely different happened.

"Oh, God! Do you see that?" he exclaimed, in awe. Looking at me with big eyes, he continued: "Something like this, I have never seen in my life!"

Well, there were many things such a young friend would never have seen, but I knew he had flown over the Channel various times. It was not his custom to wear his tongue on his sleeve and to chat about everything that went on in his mind, so I was sure what he saw was extraordinarily curious. In fact, the phenomenon increased in beauty from second to second.

"Please, come over to see my view, quickly!" he begged. "You will be amazed!"

I got up from my chair as fast as possible and looked out of his window.

"Dear Lord, what can that be?" I exclaimed, myself amazed. Even I had not seen anything so curious in my long life. The sea, which shortly before had shimmered in the most beautiful colors, had disappeared, along with the many boats which had still been moving along their colorful carpet just a few minutes prior! Something totally unknown to us had taken the place of the vast blue sea and its navy of boats.

"James! *Qu'est-ce que cela peut-être?* (James, what can that be?)" I called to him in French.

"I don't know!" James called back, astonished.

"*Moi non plus* (Neither do I)," I had to confess.

"Below all this, there must still be the sea with its many boats... don't you think?"

"Yes, they must still be there!"

"But then, what are we seeing?"

It was so new and uncommon, and beautiful beyond all measure, that at first we did not think it could be anything natural. James was as puzzled as me. He said: "It looks like shining white wool… no, like shining white snowballs!" he quickly corrected himself. "In such a great quantity!"

It expanded to all sides – far, far without any limits, a celestial countryside, dotted with millions of pearls and diamonds. It seemed unearthly soft, nothing hard or rough as in the mountains, not ragged or abysmal, but gentle elevations and valleys that were in constant motion… here bulging slightly, there plunging slowly, sometimes whirling around wildly like children. And, there we were, hurtling into this mysterious magnificence…

By and by we realized that the white objects were clouds – just as the previous clouds in which we had been enclosed and which had caused so much anxiety and fright, but these were much more benign and beautiful.

We rang for the young airplane steward, as we were convinced that he should know such spectacles of nature, and he was not only ready to help, but also rather intelligent.

"Have you got a few minutes to spare?" I asked him.

"Certainly, Sir. I am at your service."

"Can you first tell me where we are?"

"We have already crossed the Channel," he replied, "and are now flying over England towards London."

"I thought so. But now, something else: Have you seen the splendid aerial phenomenon – I mean, that beautiful shining area over which we have flown a short while ago?"

He smiled and said calmly, in a matter-of-fact tone: "Sir, you are the ninth passenger today asking me that question! Ah, but it is especially beautiful today, indeed. In fact, it never looks the same way twice. These are nothing but rain clouds. The only difference is that we are looking at them from above, from the point of view of the sun, not from the earth below or being enclosed inside them as we were some minutes ago!"

Then the little boy began to speak. He was still mystified after that fairytale-like scene, and asked: "How can rain clouds gleam so beautifully and appear so shining white?"

"Quite simply because the sun is shining directly on them," was the answer. "From beneath, on the reverse side, they look dark because of their shadow. The denser the clouds, the darker the shadow."

We thanked the helpful steward for his helpful explanation. It was the prosaic interpretation of a wonderful atmospheric phenomenon! Those mighty English rain clouds, flooded by the sun by a magical light, continued to please and fascinate us for several more minutes. That English rain cloud has shown both James and me – more than any homily – how different things can be, depending on when we see them from below or from above, or even when we get swept up into them. For James, it was sufficient that he knew the facts. However, in my mind, I recalled a hymn by which the young people of Freiburg (in the Black Forest in Germany) welcomed me once when I visited them and gave a lecture. I liked it so very much that it had stuck in my memory. It went something like this:

"If there was no night anymore / no day could exist / if there was no rain / the sun would not be bright / and there is distress to teach us / to understand joy!"

The original text – in a southern German dialect – reads as follows:

> *Wenn kein Nacht nimmer käm,*
> *Könnt kein Tag nit bestehn,*
> *Wenns kein Regen nit hätt,*
> *Wär die Sonn nit schön,*
> *Und das Leid ist wohl da,*
> *Daß wir d'Freud recht verstehn.*

Our flight allowed us a good while longer to take in the incomparable poetry of the English sun-lit clouds, until we finally approached London, the mighty metropolis of the British Empire.

The landing at the big London airport was smooth. On disembarking our plane, a big English bus took us straight into the middle of indescribable hustle and bustle.

When we got off the bus, James, my little travel companion, fell fit and fine into the hands of his relatives who had been waiting for him. He introduced me to his family, claiming that during the flight we had become good friends. They thanked me for tolerating any trouble James had caused me; of course I had to protest against that presumption, because – on the contrary – I had enjoyed his company.

We parted cordially, with me promising to make a short visit with him before I left London. As James disappeared with his relatives into the heart of London, I went by car to where my English friends were waiting for me at Southwell House in Endsleigh Street.

There I would be staying until I departed England en route to New York.

NONNI IN AMERICA

CHAPTER 16

THE GREAT LONDON MAILBOX

I was now in London, the second stop on my world trip.

Paris had been the first… Paris, the brilliant metropolis of France, regarded as one of the most brilliant and most elegant cities of the world. As I have spent many years of my life in Paris, I can confirm that is true! But, London is bigger, a world by itself… a world of grandeur and might like hardly any other city on earth.

I had visited London several times in the past and had admired some of the sights there. I was in London for the first time fifty years earlier, i.e., half a century ago! Even way back then, the splendor of that wonderful metropolis made an unforgettable impression on me. I lodged with friends in Mount Street next to Hyde Park.

I had a curious little adventure on that first day in London, fifty years ago. I will tell about it here in short, and just for fun.

On that day, I had no commitments, and wanted to stroll a bit through the city for the first time. Therefore, I turned to one of my English friends in Mount Street and asked: "This afternoon, I would like to go downtown. Please, do tell, what should I visit first?"

My friend, a cheerful man, who loved to make jokes, answered: "As you have not seen anything in London yet, I would advise you to start by going to have a look at the central mailbox of London. It is not far from here."

"The central mailbox?" I asked. "A mailbox! – Have I understood you correctly?" I was convinced that my friend wanted to fool me. But it was meant seriously, indeed.

"Yep – the central mailbox of London," repeated my friend, with true English quiet and calmness. "Just go there. You will be surprised."

I was still thinking that he only wanted to make fun, and therefore, I replied: "Until now, I have never had any special interest in mailboxes. Furthermore, I have often seen various kinds in many other cities I have visited. Aren't there any other sights which might be more interesting than that mailbox?"

"Certainly, there are many others. But, let's start with that mailbox, I suggest, being a good friend of yours. I am sure that you will be grateful to me after you have seen it. It will help you understand the other sights all the better."

There was nothing I could do. I had to give in.

I went there that afternoon, accompanied by my friend who wanted to be certain that I did not miss my goal. I wondered a lot about the peculiar care with which he planned our visit of the London mailbox. In the silence of my mind, I supposed that that mailbox was possibly part of a famous magnificent building which had been given that peculiar name. But no, amazing as it may sound, the mailbox which my friend had in mind was more or less a real mailbox, as my friend assured me. Most peculiar was the size of the mailbox, he said. My friend told me that each day, many wagon-loads of letters and packages were thrown into it. But now comes the strangest fact:

In that mailbox, he said, there lived people! Not only one person or two, but a whole lot of people! My friend told me this on our way.

At last, the horse-carriage stopped, and we got off. When my friend paid the coachman, he said to me: "Here we are. I leave it up to you to find the mailbox!" Then, he went away.

I looked around but did not see anything looking like a mailbox.

Finally, I asked a passer-by: "I beg your pardon, where is the central mailbox?"

The man pointed to a certain direction without saying anything, as Englishmen typically do.

I thanked him and went to the indicated place… but there was no mailbox to be seen!

I asked another pedestrian.

"There it is," said the man, pointing in the same direction as the first.

I went there, but only discovered a very thick and broad wall, a finely built stone wall. Into that wall, many rows of broad holes and bays had been cut in. Suddenly, I became aware of a lot of people walking up to that wall and then walking away from it. I looked closely and discovered that these people were carrying letters and packages in their hands. When they reached the stone wall, they threw the letters and packages through the respective openings. It was only then that I began to understand, and I, too, approached the peculiar wall.

I stopped next to one of the mysterious openings and had a curious look.

And what did I see?

I saw a huge subterranean hall very deep below, like a very big and nicely appointed cellar. It brought to mind the wonderful fairy tales from "A Thousand and One Nights" which I had read in my youth in Iceland. I thought of the enchanting subterranean grottoes, full of gold and silver and pearls and gems, which Arab princes and adventurers found in the mountains of Arabia sometimes.

In this big subterranean cellar, however, one did not see pearls or diamonds, nor gold or silver. Instead, I saw many people walking up and down. Everything was moving. A great many men and women picked up the letters and packages constantly being tossed through the openings in the magical wall up there on the street… letters and parcels which poured like rain into that mighty cellar, where the mail was handled in a state-of-the-art manner. I saw long, robust tables where letters were stamped continually by men doing that job with acrobatic speed.

So, this was the "central mailbox" of London! I have often thought back on that with much fondness. More importantly, I had to admit that it was quite right to say that this box was really an authentic sight to see in the huge city of London.

That happened 50 years ago.

In that next half century, many things have changed in London – and mostly for the better. This time, however, I did not see the huge central mailbox of London anymore. I do not know what has happened with it.

During my next stay in the wonderful city of London, I visited as many sights as possible. In doing so, I was struck by the fact that the external appearance of the city scape had become much prettier over the past five decades. London has become even nicer and more elegant in all aspects than it was then. The streets are impeccably clean, from the squares and uncountable public parks to the smaller idyllic gardens and greens.
Everywhere, wherever possible, flower beds are laid out and groomed with utmost care. Carriages, buses and coaches are clean and well-maintained, too. The policemen are tall, strong and polite – and especially welcoming to foreigners, like me.

NONNI IN AMERICA

CHAPTER 17

A TRIP TO THE AMERICAN EMBASSY

With that visit to London's central mailbox a half a century ago, I now had totally different business affairs to take care of. From London, I intended to cross the Atlantic Ocean and go directly to New York. That was a long stretch, and an important part of my journey around the globe. However, I discovered a great difficulty even before departure. Crossing the Atlantic would be a comparatively simple task: I only had to pay for a ticket for the trip on the big steamer "Berengaria" from England to New York. But once landing in the United States of America, however, I would not be allowed to disembark without special permit by the American government, and I had to apply for that permit at the Consulate General of the United States of America prior to my departure from London. I would need to pay for this with a substantial sum of money. This was new to me, and I would never have thought of it.

When I reached the office of the Consul General, I found a lot of people there who had the same objective: they wanted to travel to America, so they had come to pay their fees and sign various declarations. One after the other, each was received either by the Consul General or by his deputy. When it was my turn, I was accompanied to that important gentleman himself.

I greeted him and was received by him in a very polite way. "You want to travel to the United States of America?" asked me the Consul General.

"Yes, Sir."

"May I ask the purpose of your trip?"

"The purpose of my trip is very easy: I would like to get to know the American continent while visiting some friends there."

"And, why would you like to do this?"

"Because I would like to know what America is like. I have never been there."

"Why would you like to know that?"

"Because it interests me."

Now there was a pause. Apparently, the consul

did not know what else he could ask me. In order to help, I said: "I also intend to write about my observations in America."

"Fine," said the gentleman, "I shall give you the permit to stay in America for approximately 60 days."

"I thank you very much," I said. "However, I fear that 60 days will not be sufficient for me. I have planned to stay a little longer."

"Approximately how long would this be, then?"

"At the moment I cannot tell you precisely," I answered honestly, "I had in mind to stay until I finished my observations and my visits."

"Then, shall we say, four months?" he inquired. I asked, "With your permission, may it be six months? Perhaps I will not need so much time. But to be on the safe side, I would prefer six months."

"Good," said the very polite and friendly gentleman, "let's say six months. Have you enough money for a stay of six months?"
"I hope so," I answered.

He responded, "You must be absolutely sure."

"Well, then, I am sure," was my answer.

Then a strange order was given. The gentleman said: "Please go and obtain a written declaration, stating that everything you have told me here is correct, and bring it back to this office. That declaration has to be signed by a well-known person here in London." With that, the session was over.

So, I went to my friends in Mount Street and asked them why the Americans seemed so reluctant to receive travelers. They said the reason was because there were so many unemployed, and therefore poor, people in the United States. The government there did not want to increase the numbers of poor people, which was understandable. One of my London friends gave me the declaration required by the consul. I took it back, as requested, and he was satisfied. Then, I paid the required sum of money and finally obtained permission to travel to America and stay for six months.

At last, all difficulties had been removed, and the way was open to me. Shortly afterwards came the time to say good-bye. On the last day with my friends in Endsleigh Street, who had shown me such touching hospitality, the house-father came to me and said: "I have heard that you are leaving tomorrow. Is this true?"

"Yes, it is true, unfortunately. Tomorrow I travel to Southampton, where lies my boat, the "Berengaria," which will depart from England to New York."

"In that case," said the house father, "we have to celebrate your departure as best we can!"

I understood immediately that he wanted to organize something nice in order to please me. However, I asked him to refrain from that idea, for he had already done so much for me during my stay. But all begging and protesting was in vain. He said, "Herewith, I invite you to join us in a little farewell dinner this afternoon." I had to accept. The "little farewell dinner" turned out to be a first class feast! My gentle English friends and hosts in Endsleigh Street rendered me the most poignant sendoff, for which I will never be able to thank them adequately.

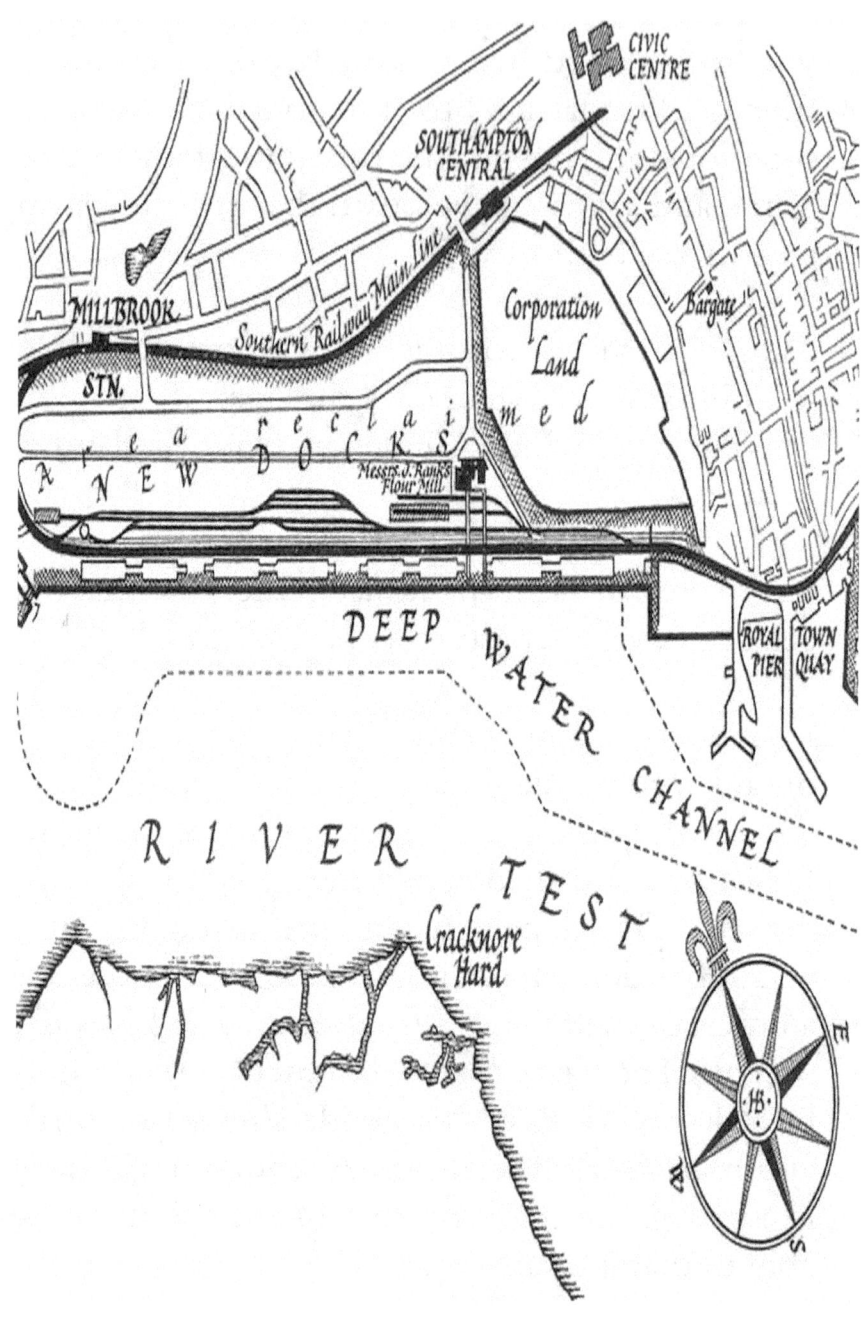

CHAPTER 18

BOARDING THE "BERENGARIA"

On August 28, 1936, I left the hospitable house in Endsleigh Street, London, accompanied by the blessings of my English friends wishing me well for my trip around the world. Going by a London train fully booked by fellow passengers heading to America, I reached Southampton around evening that same day. There, the huge steamer "Berengaria" awaited the America-bound travelers. How eager I was to see that mighty giant steamer for the first time, and then to board the boat which would cross the Atlantic Ocean and take me to New York!

To reach the city of Southampton, our train passed slowly through many suburbs until it arrived at the seashore. I looked through the window of my train compartment to see if I might spy our giant steamer "Berengaria" somewhere. All my other travel companions did the same. Yet, it was in vain; the huge boat was not seen anywhere.

We noticed that our train had reached the quay close to the seashore. Someone on the train remarked, "The 'Berengaria' has to be close by!" However, it was not visible from our viewpoint. On one side of the train there were high buildings. On the other side, strongly built bulwarks, very close to the sea.

Our train slowed considerably as it reached the destination, but we had not yet stopped. Suddenly, it became strangely dark in the train… and at the same time, we noticed a mighty towering wall before us, obliterating most of the daylight from our view.

Someone asked in the darkness: "What on earth is that pitch black monster?"

"That must be a huge building, probably a big factory," replied someone else.

What could that raven-black wall be? I asked myself.

While we speculated, the train came to a halt. The doors opened and the passengers began pouring out of the cars. As we made our way toward the mysterious, towering wall which cast its shadow on everything nearby, we discovered to our great astonishment that this was neither factory nor wall, but was really and truly our steamer, the

"Berengaria" waiting for us to board!

This ship was formerly a German vessel called "Imperator," now known as the proud English "Berengaria." I was amazed and overwhelmed …I had not imagined how huge this colossus would be. Now, here I was, up close!

The enormously long, pitch black wall was one side of the vessel, floating motionless in the water next to the bulwark. Everything around it looked tiny by comparison. It seemed that there was nothing else but the "Berengaria" alone.

Several rows of picturesque decorations ran from the front to the back alongside the amazingly long ship. They were, in actuality, uncountable small, round windows, which sailors called "bulls' eyes."

High above the hull, one could discover a lot of tiny little human heads – if you were keen-eyed. Those were the passengers that had arrived before us and had already made themselves at home aboard. They now were looking with curiosity down at us, who had arrived later.

All my fellow passengers were now standing at the quay outside the train, chatting and taking leave from their friends. They made a huge crowd, while I stood there, alone, studying all that was happening around me. As I waited, I noticed something completely new on the hull: two snow-white lines, which moved from top to bottom in a very peculiar way. I could not figure out what my naked eye was seeing. The distance to the ship was still too far. Fortunately, I had my binoculars with me. I positioned them on the peculiar white "ribbons" on the hull … and then recognized it was a great many men – all of them in snow-white clothes. Over delicate stairs called the "gangway," the white-clad men climbed down the shiny black huge hull, one after the other.

I asked a neighbor what kind of people those were and what they might have in mind. He answered:

"They are stewards who want to help us get on board with our suitcases."

"I wonder how many stewards and sailors will be on the 'Berengaria' in total?" I asked.

"Approximately eight hundred fifty."

Meanwhile the white-clad sailors came toward us and mingled in the crowd. They began to guide us forward to start boarding the huge ship. Men and women, suitcases and chests, and everything comprising the rest of our luggage – soon all were safely on top of that giant big ship.

I also wondered how many people would be on that boat. I asked one of the stewards, and he answered: "All in all, we are around two thousand five hundred passengers."

Soon afterwards I was able to confirm that number with my own eyes.

Now we were all on board ... a surging crowd on top of the deck. However, a difficult task lay ahead of us: Each passenger's passports and other documents had to be checked before we could go to our cabins. We stood about in a big herd, watched by all sides. A little further in front of us was a narrow passageway which was also surrounded by stewards, and that was the corridor through which we were to pass and show our papers. We queued up to be accepted as soon as possible as fully valid travelers to America.

NONNI IN AMERICA

CHAPTER 19

MR. GARFIELD, I PRESUME

While standing in the long queue of passengers waiting to board, it was soon clear to me that most of my fellow travelers were either English or American. I noticed this by their looks and their language and behavior. Almost all of them spoke English – some with the true English pronunciation and intonation, others with the dialect used in the United States of America.

Waiting was a real test of our patience. There we all stood, young and old, men and women, in an endlessly long procession… one person behind the other, moving toward the narrow entrance where our fates were determined by the gentlemen checking passports. Many of those waiting had the advantage of being acquainted with each other. There were small groups and parties of tourists traveling together and chatting.

I did not have that consolation. I did not know anybody, and nobody knew me. Therefore, it would not be easy for me to initiate conversation, especially with most everyone else already engaged with their companions.

That idea had barely crossed my mind when I heard somebody behind me ask: "Pardon me, Sir? You seem to be a foreigner… is this your first trip to America?"

"Yes, that is true," I answered.

The man asking was a distinguished looking, middle-aged gentleman standing directly behind me.

He continued: "you are travelling alone?"

"Yes, all alone."

"In that case," he said, "I would like to offer to be of service to you during our journey."

I could hardly believe my ears! Never in my life had a complete stranger offered me help like this, for the journey would take several days. Amazed at such generosity, I said to him: "Sir, you are much too amiable making such an offer!"

He insisted: "Oh, no, it would be my pleasure if I could be of help to you during the journey!"
Still amazed I answered, "I can only say how very grateful I am for your extraordinary friendliness! I

guess that you have made this trip between Europe and America previously?"

"Oh, yes, many times."

"In that case," I said, "your help will be greatly appreciated."

"Certainly!" he assured me. "I do know my way around!"

Thus, we began to chat, and time flew by much faster than before. My new friend turned out to be a very pleasant person to talk with. He quickly sensed which subjects interested me most and directed our conversation to those topics. He never interrupted with his own concerns. It did not seem long, then, before we reached the narrow gate where the passports and other papers were checked by the authorities on board. After our respective papers were inspected and approved, we had to separate for a short time in order to take possession of our cabins. Strangely enough, I realized we had not yet introduced our names to each other! When I had settled everything into my cabin, I went back out on the vast deck into the surging crowd strolling to and fro, joking, chatting and laughing on this magnificent ship. Occasionally I exchanged a few words with one or the other travelers passing by. All were friendly and cheerful. Still, I did not yet see my new friend to ask his name.

It was already late in the afternoon, and the weather was brilliant, mild and warm. I asked a passer-by: "Do you know when we shall depart from here?"

"Not before tomorrow morning," he answered. "We shall remain overnight here in Southampton."

After wandering around a bit more, I finally sought out a quiet corner on deck from where I would have a nice view. I sat down on a chair to contemplate the city of Southampton, as well as the English landscape behind, and the gorgeous, mirror-like ocean.

Lively passengers continued moving over the spacious deck. I was content to witness the good mood and spirits of so many happy folks chatting merrily around me. Captivated by the colorful bustle on deck of the "Berengaria," I did not notice that a gentleman was heading towards me.

When he was near, he stopped, got a chair and sat down beside me. The newcomer greeted me, then asked: "Are you traveling to New York, Sir?"

"Certainly," I answered. "Although my full journey will go on further, my first stop in America will be New York."

"It seems you are traveling with a distinguished companion, are you not?"

That seemed to me almost like a detective's question. How on earth could he know this? I felt a little shy, and answered evasively: "Until now, I have traveled completely alone. Only from Paris to London did I have a little English boy with me. He was the only companion I've had during my journey so far."

"In that case, I must beg your pardon," the gentleman said. "I thought you had a travel companion, because about an hour ago, I saw you walking next to a very distinguished gentleman. I assumed you were friends traveling together."

I began to trust a little more, so I gave him a little more detail. "The truth is, about an hour ago – as you have said correctly – I was with a gentleman whom I just met, who is travelling to New York like me. He was very friendly and amiable. Yet, I confess, I do not even know his name yet."

"Oh, is that so?" The gentleman now seemed surprised. "You do not know his name? Then I will give you his name! That gentleman is James R. Garfield!"

"Garfield!?" I repeated.

"Yea, his name is Garfield, and he lives in Cleveland …"

I interrupted. "Garfield! But, that is the name of one of the presidents of the United States of America! In fact, President Garfield was assassinated in 1881 by a furious fanatic. That crime left an immense impression on me." I continued. "I remember it vividly. I was still a young man, living in Leuven (Belgium) where I was studying philosophy. The whole world spoke with horror about that abominable crime. You say that the gentleman who spoke with me an hour ago bears that name – of all names?"

"Yes, that was certainly Mr. James Garfield you spoke with."

"This Mr. Garfield who spoke with me an hour ago… is he related to the President of the United States of America who was assassinated, with the same name?"

The gentleman looked at me amazed … and there was a short pause. Then he said: "Well, let me tell you: that gentleman you met is his son!"

I looked at the gentleman in bewildered silence. I was not yet able to believe his words… how on earth could he know this… how on earth could this be that President's son?

Puzzled, I asked: "Sir, I probably have not understood you correctly. Am I to believe that the distinguished American gentleman with whom I spoke an hour ago is the son of President Garfield?"

"Yes, indeed!" he answered. "Mr. James R. Garfield is really the son of the late President Garfield. When President Garfield was murdered, his son was just a boy of 16. Now, 55 years have passed since President Garfield's death. Your new friend, Mr. Garfield, is now 71 years old."

"And, what has become of him?" I asked.

"He is a lawyer, and lives in Cleveland, Ohio, as I said before."

It was hard to believe what this gentleman said: By coincidence, I had fallen into the hands of a famous person! And, that famous person had offered his help and advice during my journey to New York! Such tremendous luck! My latest acquaintance and I continued chatting. Suddenly, there was a loud tolling.

"That means it is dinner-time!" remarked the gentleman.

The many passengers proceeded from all sides toward the dining-room on ship. I parted ways with the friendly gentleman who had given me such interesting information and joined the crowd. On the way to the dining-room, Mr. Garfield found me and approached in greeting.

"Thanks be to God that I found you here!" he called, merrily. "I have been looking for you!"

"I am much obliged," I responded. "From now on, I will let you guide me."

"I am very glad," he replied, "and I encourage you to depend on me until we have reached New York."

I assured him I was resigned to such good fate.

"That's exactly my wish!" said Mr. Garfield. Then, he walked alongside and guided us both toward the big dining-room.

"Have you got any friends or acquaintances on board?" he asked on the way.

"No, Sir, I do not know anybody here."

"I will look for a small table, then, where we can dine calmly."

And so he did. From then on, I did not have to wonder or worry about anything, as Mr. Garfield took care to guide me about, and he did so with the utmost tact and friendliness.

CHAPTER 20

A TALE OF TWO SHIPS

After dinner I went on deck with Mr. Garfield, where we stayed for a long time. It was a pleasure talking with such an amiable companion. He was highly educated and had great experience of life. Besides that, his manner was extremely kind and thoughtful.

We strolled to and fro on deck as we chatted, taking in the lively atmosphere on board. "It's like Grand Central Station!" remarked a passenger walking by. It was true, considering how many travelers were still finding their place and collecting all their belongings. Some had lost track of their luggage on the train, at the quay, and even on the ship itself, and were searching frantically. But there was nothing to fear: being on board the "Berengaria" was like being on our own island. Nobody could take anything away and leave. Everything had its own place; one only had to stick to that principle and find that place. But even though the boat was huge, we did not feel restricted or cloistered like we might on an island.

We noticed that the ones having the greatest difficulty adjusting to life at sea were the children on board. Oh, those poor little children! Some of them did not feel well or had become seriously sick. It was difficult to bring order into their world, as evidenced by those who broke down in tears, wailing and screaming.

After a while, my dear helper and friend Mr. Garfield wished to retire to his cabin. I accompanied him there and bade him goodnight… but afterwards, I opted not to retire myself, and went on deck again. I found a quiet place where I could observe everything closely. The noise and bustle on deck diminished, little by little, until finally I was the only one sitting up there. I loved that silence, because now I could dedicate myself completely to my thoughts and dreams.

My thoughts circled around the journey at hand, which would find me tomorrow crossing the mighty Atlantic Ocean on this palatial ship. And… this trip from England to America was nothing compared with what was to follow afterwards! In fact, it was only a short stretch compared with the tremendously long world trip yet to come. I might have even been terrified of the magnitude of that idea, but being something of an experienced globetrotter already, I abstained from imagining the whole journey with all its difficulties at once. On the contrary, I decided – for the time being - to think only of the first part of my trip: the crossing of the huge Atlantic Ocean. That was enough for the moment. I expected a lot of this journey and I tried to picture what I might see or experience during that voyage.

But then I recalled another voyage almost seventy years earlier, when I was only twelve years old – the voyage from Iceland to Denmark, on the small vessel "Valdemar of Rönne." I have described that experience in my book, *Nonni*.

I began comparing both journeys in my mind – the past trip to Denmark, and this one. Back then, I was the only passenger on board the boat "Valdemar" – here, however, I was one of several thousand! On board of "Valdemar of Rönne," there were only three sailors in total; here there were 850 sailors and stewards. My former ship was so tiny that one could have compared it with a boat. The "Berengaria," however, was one of the biggest ships on earth!

NONNI IN AMERICA

My trip from Iceland to Denmark lasted five weeks. Our journey from England to America would only take five days – although the distance was so much longer.

Back then, on the small "Valdemar of Rönne" I felt fine, but there was no luxury nor comfort. Here on the royal "Berengaria," there was wealth and comfort in all aspects – a veritable land of milk and honey!

And so, I sat, completely alone, caressed by the mild air of the beautiful summer night. I sank deeper and deeper into the realm of memories and dreams. The world trip on the "Berengaria" and the adventures on the small "Valdemar of Rönne" were growing closer together, and soon they merged together in the dreams of my subconscious mind.

All of a sudden, I startled – somebody was coming down the stairs, then I heard footsteps close by. The sound echoed like the person came from a big hall, with a faint resonance. From across the deck, a high figure approached me. I remained seated and did not move. The figure came up to me and looked concerned. I was confounded and astonished, but my astonishment did not last long, for soon I recognized it was my friend Garfield!

He greeted me cordially, then asked, "You don't want to stay up here the whole night, do you?"

"Not really," I replied. "I am only sitting here in order to relax a bit. This summer night is so beautiful – I have to enjoy it a bit longer!"

"You are right!" he answered.

"Don't you want to sit down for a few moments, Mr. Garfield?"

"With pleasure, if I won't disturb you!" said the good man, sitting down on a chair opposite me.

I don't remember exactly what we talked about. I only know that we spoke about the two voyages: the one I made at the age of 12 years, and the one I was undertaking now at the age of eighty, which will lead me around the earth.

Suddenly Mr. Garfield got up and said: "I think it is time to go to bed. It is almost midnight." He pulled out his watch from his pocket and showed it to me.

Now, I wanted to get up from my seat, too… but, how strange! I was not able to stand up! It was impossible… I could not make the slightest movement, although I tried very hard.

"I will help you," said Mr. Garfield. He grasped my hands and tried to lift me, in vain. Then Mr. Garfield let loose, and I fell back… and opened my eyes.

Mr. Garfield had disappeared without a trace! Instead. there were two strong English sailors near me! Completely puzzled and with amazement, I looked at them.

Confused and helpless, I kept calling: "Mr. Garfield! Mr. Garfield! Where are you, Mr. Garfield?" The sailors smiled as if they knew what was happening.

Finally, one of them asked: "Who is Mr. Garfield?"

"That is the gentleman who was at my side up to now."

"You are mistaken, Sir! There is nobody with you, except for us," replied one of the sailors.

"But... just a few seconds ago, he was there, where you are sitting, opposite me, on that chair! And we have talked together up to now... and then he wanted to help me get up!"

The sailor repeated, "That is – as I said – an error, Sir. Only we have been here, for a long time, and during that time, you were sitting on that chair, sound asleep."

"Really?" I asked, incredulous. "Have I slept here for a long time?"

"Certainly, for quite a long time! It is already three o'clock!"

"Dear God!" I said to myself. "Then the whole thing was a dream!"

"Already, for several hours," the sailor answered, smiling. "You were sleeping when we arrived. You talked aloud from time to time."

My whole conversation with Mr. Garfield had only been a dream!

"But, why didn't you wake me up?" I asked the two sailors finally.

"Should we intrude upon your dream, Sir?" was their answer.

I thanked the sailors for having let me stay on deck in the pleasant evening air. On board everybody was long asleep – except for the sailors on watch. So, I went downstairs to my cabin, and spent the rest of the first night on the "Berengaria" sleeping healthily.

NONNI IN AMERICA

CHAPTER 21

A LITTLE ADVENTURE IN THE NURSERY

The next morning, I startled when a strong noise and heavy trembling of the hull quickly roused me from sleep. At first, I remained still in my bed and listened. The sound came from exactly above me: people trampling heavily and running around. Loud sounds like commandos could even be heard in my cabin! What on earth could it be? On top of it all, a very strong humming and drumming noise now and then drowned out the other noise. It was much too peculiar… I had to go upstairs to see for myself what all of this was.

Before I jumped out of bed, I collected myself quickly and said a short morning prayer. That was something I did each morning as I promised my dear mother I would, all the way back to the year 1870 before my departure from Iceland to Denmark. It never occurred to me not to fulfill that promise. It had become a necessity for me to say a heartfelt prayer every morning when I woke up.

When I had finished my morning prayer, I looked at my watch. It was already late in the day; but I had gone to bed quite late, after all. The other passengers had likely risen long ago. I was probably the last to arise! So, I got quickly out of bed, washed and dressed. Then, I left my small cabin and entered the lower corridor, which stretched to the left and to the right along the many cabin doors. About twenty paces away were the stairs leading upstairs to the upper deck. I made my way toward the stairs. When I had taken just a few steps, I met a sailor.

"Excuse me," I said to him, "what noise is that upstairs on deck?"

"It is the departure, Sir. We are now sailing from England to France," answered the sailor hastily as he rushed away.

I, too, continued toward the stairs. However, before reaching them, I saw a half-opened door to a large room. In taking a peek inside, I noticed it was a cute nursery! In the middle of the room there was a round, red, polished table, around which sat three silent little boys, about three to four years old. With crossed arms they leaned against the table – all three in the same fashion – looking at each other very earnestly.

They were not bothered by my entry at all. In fact, they did not even look at me, but remained seated, rigidly in the same position, staring at one another. That little group was unspeakably cute to look at, but at the same time, it was peculiar, even unnatural, for children that young to be so still. I was also astonished to realize there was nobody there looking after them. The whole situation was a riddle to me! Their silence and lack of childlike liveliness and fidgeting was troubling. After I observed them for a few minutes, I left the room and moved quickly towards the stairs, to get to the deck as soon as possible.

When I reached the bottom of the stairs, I looked up to see a small boy who looked exactly like the three boys I had just observed in the nursery. "*He must belong to them*," I thought. "*He probably took his heels, to make an excursion on his own."* But what was he doing there, on the stairs? He was caught up in his own activity, trying to slide down the stairs on his bottom. That was rather difficult, because the poor little boy was still far away from being a skilled sportsman. With great enthusiasm, he slid from step to step, but so clumsily that I was earnestly afraid the little boy would lose his balance and fall down the rather steep stairs. That could have been life threatening! I remained a few steps below to catch him, should he suddenly lose his balance. I did not have to wait long, because at that very moment he tipped over frontwards and rolled like a small ball down to the bottom of the stairs! Luckily, his clothes made a bundle of soft material. There he remained without giving the slightest sound, which told me he had not suffered a dangerous injury.

I jumped to his aid as he lay there, completely silent, a picture of misery.

Quickly, I picked him up. Hoping that his mother would come soon, I waited for a few moments at the bottom of the stairs. When nobody came, I asked the little one: "Where is your mother?"

As I did not get an answer, I tried other questions; however, it was impossible to get a single sound out of the little boy. Instead of answering, he calmly stared at me with his big, clear eyes.

Finally, I asked as friendly as possible: "Mama? Where is Mama?" This time, I was successful.

"Mama, Mama!" he repeated several times. – "Mama" belongs to the general children's language, after all. Now, we understood each other. I would go and look for his dear Mama. But first, I took the little boy through the lower passage to the nursery where I had been a short while before.

The three boys were still sitting there, exactly as before. I grabbed a small children's armchair, moved it to the table and placed my little ward on it. He did not protest, crossing his arms and resting his elbows on the table. The small, cute company at table had increased by one member. Again, they all kept still, deadly serious and immobile. My little ward mirrored their posture and seemed comfortable with them.

I left my little friends there and went up to the deck, where I saw a few English and American young ladies standing together chatting with each other. I approached the group, greeted them, and told them about my adventure with the little boy on the stairs.

"Oh! It was my little boy! Poor little Eddie!" one of the ladies cried out. "I am very thankful to you, Sir!" she added, turning towards me, and asked me to accompany her to the nursery. We went there together. When we entered, the whole small company sat quietly around the table.

The mother hugged her little son dearly, but reproached him as a mother would do for having made that excursion to the stairs after he promised to remain quietly in the nursery with his little comrades. She also examined him to make sure nothing was wrong with him after the accident. She placed the little one back in his chair and told him that she had to leave him for a short moment only, and then she would pick him up and take him to the deck.

In that instant, while I was still exchanging a few words with the young mother in the nursery, something completely incomprehensible and unexpected happened. The neighbor of our little Eddie leapt up, turned towards him, and dealt him a blow with his clenched fist, right into the middle of his face – at full strength! Fortunately, the impact was minimal, but a deafening howling was the consequence. Understandably, poor little Eddie screamed and wept in outrage!

As quick as a flash, his mother came to his rescue. She lifted him up, pressed him against her heart and tried to console him as only a mother can do. All the while, the unjust aggressor sat quietly on his chair, regarding everything that happened around him, exactly as before. At last, Eddie's desperate weeping stopped. His mother turned to the boy and asked why he hit little Eddie so hard. The boy remained mute and behaved as if nothing had happened. One could not get anything out of him.

The mother took her little Eddie with her and went to her own cabin.

Soon, the other children were also picked up by their mothers.

Thus ended the unexpected children's drama on board of the "Berengaria."

NONNI IN AMERICA

CHAPTER 22

FIRST STOP CHERBOURG

Soon I was able to get up to the deck, where I wanted to witness our grand departure. That was a rather strange adventure, beforehand, you must know.

When I arrived on the deck, I met up with my dear Mr. Garfield.

"Now we are leaving," he said.

"Yes, that's why I have come here!" I said.

The two of us went together to the top of the foredeck. From there we could observe best what was going on. As he knew everything exactly, Mr. Garfield explained each detail precisely. The most important detail was to get the huge boat in the right position to leave the port by its own power. You see, one side of the boat was moored closely at the bulwark of the long, stretched quay. Before it was able to move, it was important to turn the front of the ship away from land as far as possible, until it pointed exactly towards the open sea.

In order to get the huge hull into the right position, extremely strong ropes were fastened to the boat. The other ends of the ropes were attached to several heavy steam tugs. Those steam tugs would pull the front of the "Berengaria" from the bulwark. Those heavy, extremely solid steam tugs looked like real monsters. Mr. Garfield told me in English these were called "tuggers" or "tug-boats," designed for such pulling and extremely powerful. There were several of these so-called "tuggers" pulling simultaneously, but for a long stretch, the huge boat remained at the long quay. After a while, however, the enormously big colossus began to give in.

The small "tuggers" wheezed with all their strength. After working as hard as possible, the little monsters at last managed to break the resistance of the strong giant. The mighty ship moved to the right position and the front turned exactly towards the open sea. At that moment, the small but strong "pulling-boats" left the big ship, and the huge engines lying in the middle of the hull began to work. The whole ship was trembled and quaking for some time, but after a while, the ruckus died down and we were sailing calmly toward the open sea.

Our voyage from Europe to America through the seemingly endless Atlantic Ocean had begun, and soon, the City of Southampton and all of England lay far behind us.

We would only make one short stop at the French City of Cherbourg, where several hundred new French passengers and a lot of goods bound for America were to be taken on board.

"Do you know if we shall stay at Cherbourg for a long time?" I asked Mr. Garfield.

"We shall stay only a few hours," he replied.

"I suppose that the new French passengers will be taken on board there?"

"No, the French passengers will be transported by two steamers to the 'Berengaria' and will board on the open sea."

"Will the goods and the cargo also be shipped to us on the open sea?" I asked.

"No, Sir. When the French passengers have boarded, we shall sail into port and take on the cargo for America."

"Is that all we have to do in Cherbourg?"

"Yes, that's all. When the cargo is on board, we shall continue our voyage to America."

Now I knew what this brief stop would be like. We remained chatting on the high deck for quite a while. Mr. Garfield informed me about many useful and interesting details concerning life and customs in North America, where I would live for a few short months.

Mr. Garfield also informed me about the daily program of the "Berengaria" and invited me to join him for all our meals. I accepted with pleasure, as I could hardly have found a more pleasant and finer travel companion. He then chose a small table for the two of us in the big dining room of the "Berengaria." We would have our meals at that table over the next few days, and during the whole voyage, he saw to it that I had no lack of anything.

Meanwhile our ship sailed towards France at high speed. Soon, Mr. Garfield called my attention to the fact that two French steamers with passengers would appear shortly. As the French coast came into sight, some powerful gunshots were fired from the offshore rocky fortresses, and the two steamers appeared.

Our ship stopped immediately as the passenger ships drew up alongside our vessel.

By skillful maneuvers, our ship succeeded in the shortest possible time taking the French passengers on board in a comfortable way. Afterwards, we sailed into the port of Cherbourg, where the "Berengaria" was moored to one of the many bulwarks.

There was a whole mountain of cargo which we had to transport to America! The loading of those goods began at once. Agile French workers, among them many young people, picked up numerous chests, crates and sacks and carried them to the boat. With the help of giant cranes, everything was hauled into the ship's vast cargo hold, and the heap of goods at the quay was devoured by the enormously big "Berengaria."

In thanks for their careful work, some of the English and American passengers threw shining coins of all kinds to the swift dockworkers. A true rain of gold poured down on the good people! The younger ones caught the coins cleverly and put them into their pockets.

When the time for departure was signaled, the powerful engines began to work again. The huge ship quaked and trembled with the impetus of the drive, and then the "Berengaria" glided smoothly and calmly out of port. When she reached the open sea, the captain gave the order: "Full power ahead!" Now, our floating palace raced at astonishing and majestic speed through the massive Atlantic Ocean towards the "New World," which had been discovered for the first time around the year 1000 by the Icelander Leif Eiriksson, whose statue can be seen in Boston. This new world was first named "Markland," but that was forgotten until the land was discovered a second time, four hundred years later, by Christopher Columbus [who had been to Iceland and read the Sagas about Leif Eiriksson's voyage], when it received its final name, "America."

In five days, I would step into that magical New World!

CHAPTER 23

THE LITTLE AMERICAN

It was only upon departing France that I truly felt my great journey around the globe was in full swing. I was not just on a normal steamer taking me from one European country to another, as had happened before many times… no, this time it was quite different: I had begun a long trip which would take me from one continent to another, from old Europe to a young world, the American continent!

That magnificent realization had an uplifting and enchanting effect on both my spirit and my imagination. I wanted to enjoy the exhilaration of the moment, so I sought out a place on deck where I could be alone. I sat down on a bench and dedicated myself to my poetic mood.

My reverie did not last long, however, because soon I was startled by approaching footsteps.

"*That will be my friend, Garfield,*" I thought. But I was wrong. As the steps came nearer, a little English-speaking boy appeared in front of me. During the last two days, I had seen him several times in the crowd. He was about twelve years old. Each time I saw him, he made a good impression on me, as he was polite, well-educated, friendly and talkative.

Now, he looked at me for a moment, took off his cap, and said: "Good day, Sir!"

I greeted him in a short manner, too, because I thought that he was only passing by. However, he said to me in a very polite way, "Sir, may I ask you what time it is?"

I got my watch out of the pocket and showed him what time it was. He thanked me.

Then I asked him: "I suppose you are an English boy?"

"No, Sir, I am American."

"Well, well. You are American, but you asked me what time it was. I thought that all American boys had a watch."

"That is true, Sir. I do have a watch, but it has stopped. I forgot to wind it up."

"You may wind it up now, and set it by my watch. It is right, you know."

The little American obeyed immediately.

While he was setting his watch, I asked him: "Are you from the United States?"

"Yes, Sir,"

"From which city?"

"From New York," he replied. Then he asked me: "Are you also going to New York, Sir?"

"Yes, certainly," I answered. "I am going to stay in New York for a while."

He nodded. "I am pleased! You will surely like New York."

"That's what I think, too," I said. "About how many citizens live in New York?"

"Ten million, Sir! It is the biggest city – not only in America, but in the whole world!"

I smiled, because I had heard that Americans love to say that. I replied to the little boy: "What a great number of inhabitants! In that case, New York would even be bigger than London."

"Oh, yes, Sir, that is true. London is only the second largest city."

"I do believe you, my little friend… although, the Londoners say that their city is the biggest."

"Yes, that's what they say. But New York has grown faster than London."

"True… but, does New York have as many splendid buildings as London?"

"Yes, I think so," answered the boy. "At least, the big buildings in New York are much higher than those in London."

"I have heard about them. Do you know how many floors the highest buildings in New York have?"

He answered, "The tallest building in New York is the Empire State Building, which has 102 stories."

"That is a great height! Such buildings cannot be found in Europe, nor anywhere in the world. Have you ever been on top of that immensely high building?" I asked.

"Yes, Sir, several times," was his response. He continued: "I have also been on the Eiffel Tower in Paris, which is 300 meters high, but not quite as high as the Empire State Building. Nor has London any taller buildings!"

I smiled again. "You are right, my little friend. The Americans can be proud of their tall buildings, just as the Englishmen can be proud of their huge ships."

"Yes," admitted the American boy, "we hardly have any such big and beautiful ships as, for instance, the 'Berengaria,' but by and by, I bet we shall surpass the Europeans in that field, too."

I was amazed at this boy's patriotism, self-confidence and self-assurance. Suddenly, he was called by someone on the lower deck. He excused himself politely, saying that he had to go, and taking leave from me with these words: "I will gladly see you again, Sir, if you will allow me."

"You are always welcome, my little friend," I replied.

Then, he made a bow and rushed down the stairs leading to the next deck where his family was waiting for him.

Meanwhile the huge ship glided through the water at great speed.

Huge swarms of seagulls circled around the boat. Many passengers stocked up with bread to throw pieces into the air. Immediately, these snow-white birds caught them, quickly and greedily devouring them in the air. The gulls showed off their flying skills, touching the passengers on deck with their wings now and then.

The American boy with whom I had conversed did occasionally pass by, greeting me in a friendly way or sitting down next to me to talk in his childlike way about his fatherland, of which he was very proud.

Once he pointed to the seagulls and said: "At the moment, the gulls are still following our boat, but after two days they will leave us."

"Where will they fly then?" I asked him.

"They will fly back to the English coast."

"Why will they do that?" I asked again.

"Because they do not like flying so far over the open sea. They must have had a bad experience! I would guess they find more food along the coast, and that they feel safer there. They must also like to rest on firm ground from time to time."

"After the seagulls have left, will any other birds come near our ship?"

"Oh, yes," replied the little American boy. "When the seagulls leave, other birds will come and join us."

"What sort of birds?" I asked.

"They are called coots. Those are black birds, a bit smaller than the seagulls."

I must say, I was astonished by the little boy's knowledge. He entertained me in a pleasant way.

Besides my friend, there was a variety of activities on the "Berengaria". For instance, on the second day of our voyage, I walked through a long corridor on the lower floor. All of a sudden, I heard voices and a lot of laughter. Slowly, I approached the place from where the noise seemed to come. I reached a door with iron fittings. I paused for a few moments to discern what was really happening behind there. After some consideration, I opened the door slowly and stood admiringly in the doorway. What did I see? A splendidly outfitted indoor swimming pool, filled with the purest looking water!

A man standing near the pool asked me if I wanted to take a sea bath.

"A sea bath?" I exclaimed with amazement.

He pointed and said: "This pool is filled with pure, warm sea water. Here you can have a bath every day!"

"I shall have to do so!" I replied. "But first I would like to have a look around the pool."

For a while I observed the magnificent arrangements. Around the large basin, there were beautiful galleries with elegant colonnades, several meters above the water. There were many men in bathing suits. Some of them were swimming in the spacious pool, while others climbed elegant spiral staircases to the galleries, from which they dove head over heels into the deep water. All could swim to their hearts' content in the crystal-clear pool. Of course, I would not miss such an opportunity to take an invigorating bath in sea water!

The same day, I had another interesting adventure: all male passengers were ordered to go on deck. We gathered up there with sailors, together with their officers.

On deck, there were piles of rescue equipment, lifebelts, a rucksack made of thick and heavy cork, and many other things. Various items were distributed among us. The cork boards were attached to our chests and backs. Afterwards the lifebelts had to be fastened around our bodies.

In such outfit, we had to practice getting into the lifeboats. The original plan was to lower us alongside the outer wall of the ship until we reached the water level; however, they skipped that maneuver.

At the conclusion, they told us very earnestly to remember that place on the ship and the location of the life boats, so that in case of an actual emergency, we would be able to find our position.

CHAPTER 24

DAILY LIFE ON THE "BERENGARIA"

Daily life on board the luxury steamer "Berengaria" followed a usual routine. The glorious vessel sped constantly forward, with amazing speed. We were carried not only by wind and waves, but pushed forward by mighty engines, the huge vehicle cutting through the masses of water from Europe towards North America, racing with unsettling haste, over each of the five days and five nights.

Peace among the passengers was not disturbed by any exciting events. However, everyday life had so many little surprises that our time on the "Berengaria" was never boring. Besides, everything is different on such a ship, compared to the world elsewhere. Here is one example:

Before I started my journey around the globe, I made sure to buy a good watch. The days of the journey in Paris and London found it working perfectly, always precisely on the minute. It worked equally well on the "Berengaria" – but only for the first day. After that, it behaved rather strangely, all at once. It seemed once we left England and France, and had reached the Atlantic Ocean, the watch was no longer precise nor reliable.

Our second evening on board, Mr. Garfield said to me: "Breakfast is at eight-thirty every morning. I shall expect you tomorrow at eight-thirty in the dining room at our reserved table."

I promised Mr. Garfield to be punctual. "You can rely on me. I shall see you tomorrow at eight-thirty, at our table," I assured him.

The morning came and my watch showed eight-thirty. I entered the dining room… but, to my astonishment, there was not a single soul there yet, and the many small tables had not even been laid! I went to our reserved small table, sat down and waited.

After I had waited for a while – completely alone – I began wondering about the lateness of my fellow passengers and that of the personnel on board. It was already nine o'clock and breakfast should have begun at eight-thirty!

At last I heard steps outside in the passage. The door opened and a waiter entered. When he saw me sitting at my table, he approached and said: "Sir, you have come a bit too early for breakfast. Now it is only eight o'clock; breakfast begins at eight-thirty."

"I knew that breakfast begins at eight-thirty", I replied, "but my watch shows nine o'clock already. How come?"

The waiter smiled and said: "Very simple, Sir. Last night, you probably forgot to set your watch back by one hour. You need to do that every evening until we are in New York."

I made big eyes, for that was new to me. Nobody had told me that!

The waiter noticed my embarrassment and smiled: "Sir, you are not the first to not know that rule."

"I believe that!" I replied. "I thank you for informing me!"

Then, I set my watch back by one hour as the waiter had told me.

Of course, the matter was clear to me at once: Although we rushed with great speed from east to west, so did the sun, too. Thus, sunset was delayed for us, and more so, sunrise, for the earth is a globe. That delay amounted to one hour each day, which is why we had to set our watches back by one hour each day.

Soon everything was ready for breakfast. By and by, the passengers arrived and quickly filled the dining-room. Mr. Garfield was there soon, and looked after me as usual.

After breakfast I went with him on deck. We sat down and chatted while the little black and grey coots, which had come after the seagulls left, were swarming around the ship.

"I assume you came a bit too early to breakfast," said Mr. Garfield after he was seated.

"Yes," I said, "a whole hour too early! But, it did not matter."

"Nevertheless, I am sorry that I forgot to remind you of it yesterday. During the voyage to America, you have to set back your watch by one hour every evening."

"Yes, the waiter told me the same."

"But now, another question", Mr. Garfield said pulling a newspaper out of his bag. "Have you got the latest news?"

"How can one get a fresh newspaper here in the middle of the Atlantic Ocean?" I asked, astonished.

Mr. Garfield explained, "Here on board, a newspaper is printed every day. It is called 'Ocean Times,' and it can publish the latest news from all over the world, as heard via radio."

"That is quite interesting!" I replied. "Up to now, I have not seen this newspaper."

Mr. Garfield rang the bell, and a waiter rushed over to us.

"Please," said Mr. Garfield, "bring us the latest newspaper."

The waiter disappeared. After a few minutes he came back with the 'Ocean Times' and handed it to Mr. Garfield.

We perused it. I was impressed at how comprehensive it was. One could inform oneself about the latest events in the whole world. When we had finished the newspaper, Mr. Garfield said: "Tonight, in the big hall amidships, a nice historic movie will be shown. I would be very pleased if you allow me to accompany you there."

I accepted the kind offer with pleasure. And thus, we met again the same evening at the presentation of the movie. We enjoyed the film very much. But, the evening did not end without an accident… and, the poor man to whom the accident happened was me!

Not all the chairs in the auditorium were in perfect condition. The very chair which I sat on seemed to be a bit shaky from the beginning. I asked myself if it was reliable, but I felt ashamed of such fainthearted thoughts and dismissed them. Everything else on this ship seemed perfect and solid; why should my chair be an exception?

I sat down, bravely, and full of confidence.

In the beginning everything was fine.

But then, in the middle of the movie, there was an exciting scene, and the audience was naturally set in motion. Suddenly, my unfortunate chair had a dizzy spell and fell completely apart, making a big noise as it broke! I fell to the ground with the chair and sat on a heap of ruins. My friend, Mr. Garfield, helped me to get up, and a charitably minded soul provided me with a new chair. As a souvenir of that pleasant event, I kept a few bruises, but all the more vivid is my memory of that historic movie on the "Berengaria."

NONNI IN AMERICA

CHAPTER 25

A CHARMING SUMMER NIGHT

The following day on board, Mr. Garfield invited me to meet an extremely interesting company of fourteen Americans – one lady and thirteen gentlemen - who had undertaken a journey from America to Russia. They wished to experience that huge empire firsthand, as one cannot get to know such a place completely through books and maps. I felt immediate affection for them, as they had the same wanderlust as me and shared my opinion that one can only fully comprehend foreign countries and people if you go in person. They all had the same love of the unknown as I do; but, like me, they also loved their home country, to which they were now returning.

Their journey had become the center of discussion among passengers. The group was thus invited to give a talk about their impressions, and it was their pleasure to do so. We gathered in one of the many small salons and listened with great interest to this small travel group's report from Russia. Every aspect of their talk was fascinating and informative to me, as I feel the more countries and people you get to know, the better one can understand each country and each person – and even yourself and your own home country, as has become quite clear to me over my long life and many journeys throughout the world. That is the chief reason I have taken so many trips, and that is why I love to share stories about my home country of Iceland wherever I have the opportunity.

Mr. Garfield grew tired over the course of the talk, and soon left in order to rest a bit. I remained in my seat, and other Americans soon entered the salon to find their spots. Shortly, something strange and pleasant happened. A newcomer sat next to me, where Mr. Garfield had ben. He greeted me and asked: "You are traveling to my fatherland, America? May I ask you where you come from?"

"Of course, Sir, you may!" I answered. "I was born in a country which is, by far, much smaller than your fatherland. It is an island exactly between America and Europe."

When he heard that he looked at me with big eyes, and asked with great interest, "Could it possibly be Iceland?"

"You have guessed right!" I said. "It is Iceland!"

He asked: "Are you really a native Icelander?"

"Yes, Sir, I am a true Icelander."

Upon that he looked at me attentively, shook my hand, and said: "I am very pleased to meet a real Icelander here, because I am very interested in Iceland and the Icelandic people."

I must admit, I was amazed to see such unusual interest by an American towards my small home country. I was not used to foreigners finding my home country of any particular interest. In general, people do not know much about the small island in the North Sea, and even less about the Icelandic people. It has seemed, in my experience, that mostly the young people know and love Iceland, as they do not judge other countries and nations by the benefit they get from them. I recall the French youth, among whom I grew up, being like this; I also think of the German youth who have received my books and stories enthusiastically. These youth have made it possible that my Nonni books, telling of the wonders of my home country, might be translated into many cultures and languages, reaching the youth in England, Austria, Switzerland, in Luxemburg and the Netherlands. I suspect I will see similar interest among the youth of America, and then the youth in Japan, all of whom await my arrival.

By contrast, the so-called "big world," the adult political realm, usually regards Iceland as an outsiders' country at the edge of civilization. For that reason, I was astonished that this American gentleman held such extraordinary interest in my homeland. His subsequent words were full of praise, affection and appreciation for my fellow Icelanders and about my fatherland, that tiny nation up there close to the polar circle. It left me utterly astonished!

Furthermore, as the American gentleman continued, he implored me to give a proper speech about Iceland and Old Norse culture and literature, particularly Edda, the Sagas and skaldic poems originating in Iceland. He was aware that, in that old Icelandic literature, the daily life of the old Germans, from birth to death, is described much more clearly and completely than even in Tacitus. As more travelers joined us, he urged me to tell them about the old Scandinavian Vikings, the Viking raids, the discovery of countries by the Normans and their conquests around the world; and, about the discovery of America by an Icelander, some several hundred years before Columbus. My American listeners had a remarkably sound knowledge of America's discovery by Icelanders. One man interrupted me, saying: "In several American cities are huge statues of those first discoverers."

The American gentleman next to me, the one with special interest in Iceland, said: "I am quite impressed with the level of literary education and the arts found in the small Icelandic nation." He added: "I know the Icelandic sculptor Einar Jonsson personally. He lives in Reykjavík, and is regarded one of the most talented sculptors living now. I have often had contact with him and have great esteem for him."

"Then, you have been in Iceland yourself?" I asked.

"No, Sir, I met Einar Jonsson in America, when several years ago he was appointed to create a colossal statue of the Icelandic sailor Thorfinn Karlsefni in Philadelphia. Thorfinn Karlsefni is said to be the first white man who settled in America for good."

"Indeed, all the old Icelandic reports say the same," I agreed.

"And that is also recognized as a proven historic fact," he added.

"How do you like the statue of Thorfinn Karlsefni?" I asked.

"I like that statue very much! Experts say it is a first-class masterpiece. It stands in Fairmont Park in Philadelphia."

"Do you know his work, 'Queen Victoria as Empress of India'?" I continued.

He answered: "Yes, I know that very well, too. It is another masterpiece beyond all praise."

I was dearly pleased to hear such great praise given to my compatriot by strangers out here on the Atlantic Ocean… even more so, because the great sculptor was not only my compatriot, but also a dear friend of mine. I was not used to anyone understanding the small Icelandic nation as did this American gentleman – and, a complete stranger, at that!

"Do you know this Mr. Einar Jonsson?" the American gentleman asked me now.

"Oh, yes," I answered. "I met him in Copenhagen, when he was still a very young man."

"Was he already a famous artist at that time?"

"No, at that time he was not yet known. He had just arrived in Denmark from Iceland, young and penniless, with only a firm faith in his talent and ability! He settled in Copenhagen and managed to get a very small studio, where he began his work."

"What work did he do there?"

"Perhaps you have heard of 'The Outlaw,' a splendid project which was bought by a noble and rich Italian aristocrat, who paid him very well.

With that one piece, Einar Jonsson became famous."

"Yes, 'The Outlaw' is known to me," the American gentleman said.

"In that case, I would like to know your opinion!" I replied.

"With pleasure!" he said. "That most beautiful work depicts an outlaw loaded with a double burden: the corpse of his young wife, who passed away shortly before, and his little child. The man promised his wife that he would bury her in consecrated earth. Beside the man we see his dog. Both man and dog look sorrowful but determined as the outlaw risks his life to bury his bride, for anyone recognizing him would beat him to death with no repercussions. The grouping wonderfully and accurately conveys the drama of the actual ancient Icelandic event, and the sculpture has rightly earned undivided applause everywhere."

"Soon afterwards," I said, "Einar Jonsson received several honorable and promising commissions by which he not only became famous, but also completely independent. His grateful fatherland built a museum in Reykjavík in his honor. He still lives there, amidst his numerous works, which increase in number constantly."

The gentleman shook my hand and said: "We may all congratulate you on your great compatriot Einar Jonsson. Although the Icelandic nation is small, it has a great number of many important men in literature and art. Another who sheds much glory on your Icelandic homeland, in the same vein, is the immortal Bertel Thorvaldsen."

Somebody nearby interrupted: "Thorvaldsen was an Icelander? I always considered him to be a Dane."

"Thorvaldsen was a true Icelander," answered the American gentleman. "He is the son of an Icelandic wood carver. He was born in Denmark in 1768 and died in 1844, and that's why many people think he was a Dane. He himself, however, always appeared as an Icelander." The gentleman went on: "For example, he dedicated one of his works to his Icelandic compatriots while he lived in Rome. It was a splendid baptismal font of white marble held by an angel. The dedication, which Thorvalden coined himself and engraved in the marble, reads as follows: '*Opus hoc Romae fecit, et Islandiae, terrae sibi gentilitiae, pietatis causa donavit Albertus Thorvaldsen anno MDCCCXXVII.*' [Bertel Thorvaldsen created this work in Rome and dedicated it to Iceland in the year 1827 as token of his love]. This precious font was placed in front of the main altar in the Cathedral of Reykjavík."

Soon it was time for all of us to go to bed, as it had become late. Our small company dispersed, bidding each other good-night, and most retired to their cabins. I lingered a bit on deck, looking out over the sea. I saw that the night was not pitch black, but unusually bright and shiny. I went up to a higher deck in order to enjoy that splendor even more. When I had reached the uppermost deck, at first I stood still, speechless, full of admiration. What I saw up here surmounted everything I might have expected.

An indescribable silence had fallen over the huge ship as we sped forward, as well as on the immeasurable shining ocean, extending to all sides without limits. The splendor of the cloudless dome of the sky was divine. The magic of that incomparable summer night's view was so great that I could not bear to descend to my cabin. So, I sat down on a chair and marveled at the splendor of the uncountable stars gleaming with indescribable brilliancy on the nocturnal sky. At the same time, I beheld the limitless surface of the Atlantic Ocean, mirroring the whole celestial splendor, appearing in a miraculous way to beam the light back into the farthest reaches of space.

There I sat for quite some time – completely on my own – and gave myself over to the sweet feeling which that overwhelming spectacle evoked in my soul.

It was only then that I fully understood how God could say on the sixth day that everything he had created was good - after he had finished creation.

After a long while, I knew I had to leave the wonders of that singularly beautiful summer night and the blissful delight it bestowed on me. I got up and returned to the lower part of the ship, and went to my cabin. The experience on deck brought me to my knees. I knelt in front of my bed and said my evening prayers exactly as I had done aboard the small boat "Valdemar of Rönne" seventy years earlier. After all, I had promised my mother to do so during my whole life. The enchanting mood which had seized me on deck kept me awake for quite a while. Finally, however, I drifted off into the land of dreams, softly, without noticing.

CHAPTER 26

AMERICA IN SIGHT

With the long stay on deck that wonderful summer night, I had gotten to bed very late. For that reason, I slept far into the next morning. Finally, however, I was roused from my deep slumber by an unusual noise outside in the gangway immediately in front of my cabin.

I rubbed my eyes and sat up in bed.

What is this about? I asked myself. I remained still to try and hear better. Outside my door, a loud conversation was going on.

"Where could he be?" a high-pitched boy's voice asked.

"I don't know," replied an adult's low, bass voice.

"Haven't you seen him yet this morning?"

"No, not yet."

I continued listening…

"Where is his cabin?" asked the young voice eagerly.

"It is quite nearby," replied the adult.

There was a pause, and then footsteps came towards my door.

"May I open the door?", asked the boy.

"No, that is not done here," answered the adult.

It was clear that someone was looking for me. I had no idea who that was and what he had in mind, but now I got out of bed and dressed quickly. After hurriedly tidying myself, I wondered what would happen next.

For a while, I could still hear the boy asking for me, and the adult giving evasive answers. When the conversation finally stopped, I opened the door and entered the gangway. I saw there one of the sailors on duty, and next to him the little American boy whom I had met a few days earlier. As soon as the boy spied me, he came rushing towards me.

"Ah! There you are!" he shouted joyously. "I have been looking for you for quite some time!"

"So, so, you were looking for me, little friend? It must be something very important you have to tell me."

"Yes! Last night, we reached American waters! When I got up this morning, you could see the coast, using binoculars, only from a long distance."

"That is great news!" I said. "How nice of you informing me. Many thanks!"

"But, that is not everything," added the little American boy. "In a short while, we shall see New York!"

"Are you sure? Is that possible? Are we already close to New York?"

"Yes, and probably we shall even enter the city today!"

"Enter New York today! Your hometown… the biggest city of the world! How wonderful!"

"Yes, and I will explain to you everything we can see from the ship." I was highly surprised by the touching thoughtfulness of the dear little boy.

"Have you really got time for that, little friend?"

"Oh yes! My parents give me permission!"

So, everything was in order. I had to accept this friendly offer by such a charming little American!

"How long will it take, approximately, until we shall reach the port of New York?" I asked.

"It will still take several hours," my friend replied.

"Fine then. I will get ready to have a look at the coast of America together with you, and later, I shall have a look at New York."

As I still had to settle a few things, I asked the boy to come back in about an hour. With that agreed upon, I shook the good boy's hand saying: "See you soon!"

"Goodbye, Sir!" said the little one, shaking my hand in return. Then he hurried upstairs on deck.

I entered my cabin in order to get ready. I still had a few things left to do. When I finished, I rushed to the breakfast room. There, I met Mr. Garfield, who was with some noble English, American and Japanese gentlemen.

Mr. Garfield introduced us. I had the honor to meet Mr. H.G. Summerford, Admiral of the English Navy, as well as Professor Phillips Bradley from Amherst College, Massachusetts. When Professor Bradley learned that I was an Icelander, he gave me a letter for a compatriot of mine, Mr. Leifur Magnusson, International Labor Office in Washington.

Shortly afterwards, Mr. Garfield introduced me to an extremely amiable gentleman, Lord Addington, one of the leading persons in the English Oxford Movement. Next, he introduced me to a noble Japanese gentleman from Tokyo, who was very friendly and invited me to visit him and his family as soon as I arrived there.

After some time, my little American friend appeared to take me on deck. Now, I was to see, under his guidance, the American coast – for the first time in my life! I would surely marvel at the wonders of the largest city of the world as we entered the Port of New York. Thus, the young American accompanied me up all the stairs to the top deck of the "Berengaria".

En route, we encountered the mothers of the four little boys from the nursery, whose story I related earlier. This time, the little ones were not sitting around the table, but were carried peacefully in their mothers' arms. They stretched out their small hands towards me, smiling. I shook the hand of the one who was closest to me. Immediately he grasped my index finger, holding it so tightly that I had great difficulty to free myself again! The little rascal who had hit his comrade earlier was there, too, in the arms of his mother. I asked her if he had made peace with his comrade. "Oh, yes," she replied, "they are all good friends again. However, the reason for that attack is still his secret!"

I took leave of the ladies and continued my walk under the guidance of my young leader. When we reached the uppermost deck, we found many passengers there. Several had never seen America before – just like me. There was a certain serious and solemn atmosphere. My little guide was practical and clever like most Americans, and he was able to find a pleasant and convenient place from which we had the best view ahead. There, we sat down on a bench.

My young friend asked me to look straight ahead... I did so, and detected in a long distance, deep on the horizon, a dark line which came clearly into focus ... a peculiar strip, which seemed to rise from the ocean.

"There," I said, pointing, "I can see a dark line winding itself to the left and to the right on the water. On the upper part it seems to have strange curves and humps. What can that be?"

"That is America!" said the little boy.

We both looked in that direction ... and there was a solemn pause. By that first sight of a barely visible line on the horizon, far away, I could not yet draw any conclusions of that mysterious New World. But the fact that I had seen with my own eyes the tiny beginning of something quite big and important, moved me quite deeply! Yes, now I could truly say that I had finally seen the immense American continent – even if it was a tiny strip along the horizon. Now, I felt that Europe lay far behind us, and that a new, mysterious world was rising in front of our eyes, in marvelous view, emerging majestically from the ocean. It felt like I had already stepped forward into the new world!

NONNI IN AMERICA

NONNI IN AMERICA

CHAPTER 27

MY LITTLE AMERICAN GIVES A SPEECH

My little American friend and I looked for the best spot up there on the highest deck to view the American coastline, that New World which we were approaching steadily; the "Berengaria" was heading there with full power.

"Don't you have any binoculars?" I asked the boy.

"No, Sir", he replied, "but my mother has a pair of good pocket binoculars. Shall I go ask her to lend them to us?"

"No, no. She should keep hers. I myself have a pair of good binoculars which I bought before the voyage. They will do."

I took my glasses out of their pocket and handed them to the boy.

"Have a try and look if they are good indeed."

He placed them before his eyes and positioned them towards the country.

"Oh, these are really fine binoculars!" he cried out like a connoisseur. "Where did you find them?"

"I bought them a short while ago in Nauheim, where I had a spa treatment."

The boy was right: the binoculars from Nauheim were excellent.

Our approach was steady, and soon we did not need the help of my binoculars anymore. The countryside around New York was little different from what I knew in Europe: meadows and woods, small elevations and hills. Even the young American drew my attention to that fact saying: "What is special here is not this countryside, but the City of New York, which we shall see soon. You must only have a little bit of patience until we get closer to the City." And he added: "New York is one of the most beautiful cities of the whole world."

"Yes, I do believe you," I answered. "In Europe, I have heard people say that many times, and I am pleased to have the opportunity to see the beauties of New York for myself. What can you tell me about the size of this wonderful city?"

"It is difficult to give an exact number of citizens living in New York. However, it has enough space for ten million people."

I was amazed that the 12-year-old boy knew all these details, and that he was able to talk about them as reasonably as an adult. I asked him: "Where did you learn all this? And how can you remember it so well?"

"I have learned it at school," he answered. "We have to know these facts without fail."
Then he continued: "We also learned that New York cannot expand on either side because the city is surrounded by water and densely populated settlements. As the city is already full, with more and more streaming in, the city council decided to look for more space in the only possible direction

that is still free – that is, upwards! And thus, they have started to build very tall structures. In school, they told us the Germans call these tall buildings '*Wolkenkratzer*'. The French call them '*gratte-ciel*'."

"And, do you know how tall these '*Wolkenkratzer*' are?" I interrupted the boy.

"Yes, Sir, I do!" replied the little boy from New York. "Some of them are 330 feet high, others 650, but the tallest is more than 900 feet high, namely, 1,247 feet high!"

"Are you sure those numbers are correct?" I asked. "Even higher than the Eiffel tower in Paris, which was said to be the highest building on earth up to now? Can that be true?"

"Yes, it is true! In Europe they do not build such tall buildings, but in America they do. The highest building in New York, 'The Empire State Building,' is 1,247 feet high."

"That is 380 meters high! For us Europeans, that seems almost incredible!"

He promised, "You can believe it's true."

I said, "Tell me all about this wonderful building!"

After thinking a bit, he answered: "You wish to hear more details about the Empire State Building? Then, I shall tell you what I have seen with my own eyes, for I have often been up in that huge building, and I have looked at everything from top to bottom very thoroughly. The Empire State Building is definitely the tallest building of the entire world. It has 102 floors. Each floor is 11 feet high. Many thousands of people can live in those 102 floors. The higher floors are not built with stones but constructed with a much lighter material."

Here I interrupted the boy and asked him: "Do you know what that lighter material is called?"

"Yes, it is called 'aluminum.'"

"Can you tell me why the higher floors were made from aluminum, and not from stones like the floors below?"

"Because the whole building would have become too heavy. The lower floors would not be able to bear the pressure from the top of the immensely high building. They would be crushed by the heavy weight. That's what our teacher told us. The first 1050 feet are apartments, where people live. Then comes a 200-feet-high 'superstructure' which houses an observatory."

I was more and more astonished by that little American boy: how certain he was, and how well he was able to report it all. It was a real pleasure listening to him.

When he paused, I asked him the following question: "Everything that you have told me is extremely interesting. But tell me this: what can I do if I want to visit a friend who lives up there on one of the highest floors in one of those buildings? How does one climb to the top floors?

It must be rather tiring, mustn't it? In order to get to the 102nd floor, the stairs would have at least 2600 steps!"

He replied: "Stairs? That would not make much sense. For getting to the top, and descending down to the bottom, stairs have long been abolished in American skyscrapers. For such trips, electrical cars are used."

"Incredible! This gets better and better!" I cried out. "So, when someone on the lower floors wishes to visit a friend who lives on one of the top floors, he rides a car in order to reach him?"

"Yes, Sir," continued the boy, calmly. "It works rather well and is very easy. You get used to it quickly. The electrical cars in the skyscrapers are quite different from the trains running through countries. Skyscraper cars only operate upwards and downwards, and they run constantly between the bottom and top floors. We call them 'lifts' or 'elevators.' They are operated by lady attendants.

NONNI IN AMERICA

At each stop, a whole army of girls in beautiful uniforms is ready to accompany you!"

He went on: "There are as many stops as there are floors. Elevator cars stop at each station as required. But there are also direct elevators, like express trains, which operate from the bottom floor to the top without stopping."

"You have explained everything to me quite clearly, and in great detail, thank you!" I said to the little American boy. "I will be sure to visit that highly interesting Empire State Building and have a good look at everything you have mentioned. I shall use the elevator cars upwards and downwards, and also make stops in between. You have made me very curious to see them myself!"

The clever boy assured me: "I can tell you now that you will be astonished how nice, practical, and well everything has been set up there."

Now we both paused to muse a bit. I looked out toward where that wonderful city would appear before our eyes, but we were still too far away to see anything of New York.

Suddenly, the boy said: "So far, we have only spoken about the skyscrapers in New York; but they are not the only sights of the city! There are many others still which are extraordinarily beautiful and interesting."

I looked at him, quizzically. He became vivid and said: "Have you ever heard anything about New York's bridges?"

I answered, "No, not yet."

"That's strange," said the boy. "You should visit at least one of them while you are in New York, for that one is the most beautiful and the biggest bridge in the world."

"What is the name of that bridge?" I asked.

"That is called the Triborough Bridge. And, as I said, it is by far the biggest and most beautiful bridge in the whole world."

"Do you know how long it is?"

"Yes, it has a total length of 17 English miles."

"Seventeen English miles! That means more than 27 kilometers! Do you have any idea how much that immensely long bridge cost to build?"

"Certainly, I know that, too: it cost sixty million dollars."

"Sixty million dollars…!" I was amazed.

He repeated, "Yes, sixty million."

"Are you sure?"

"Yes, I am absolutely sure. Our teacher told us so, and all the newspapers reported about it."

"That is amazing, indeed! Sixty million dollars! In German money, that would be approximately two hundred and forty million marks – indeed, a huge sum! By all means, I must see this bridge while I am in New York. You are right, my little friend; such a bridge must be worth seeing."

"Well, I have to say," added the little boy quickly, "that at the moment, an even bigger bridge is being built. It will be finished in a few months."

"Pardon me – a newer, even bigger bridge? Is the Triborough Bridge not enough for New York?"

"The bigger bridge is not being built in New York," replied the little boy, "but at the other side of the United States, in San Francisco, in the state of California, at the coast of the Pacific Ocean."

I remarked, "How good that it is being built in California. I will see it there then, because during my journey to Japan I will be traveling through California, and I will stay in San Francisco for a couple of months."

Thus, we chatted on the top deck while our ship approached the American miracle city. At long last, the signal for lunch was given, and we got up and went towards the dining room. There we parted ways: the boy joined his mother, and I went to the table where Mr. Garfield was already sitting.

Mr. Garfield was as amiable as always.

"Today, we shall probably reach New York and leave the ship," I told him.

"Yes, this afternoon we shall reach New York," he said. "But we shall not be able to leave the ship yet. We will have to stay on board of the 'Berengaria' tonight. Only tomorrow will we be allowed to leave."

I asked him the reason for the long wait. "There are several reasons," he answered. "New York is very big, and the passage to our ship's berth is long. Besides that, there are several formalities with which all passengers have to comply, including a health check. All that takes time."

I knew the delay could not be helped. We had to comply with those regulations. I would make the most of my time on the ship, nevertheless.

NONNI IN AMERICA

CHAPTER 28

FIRST SIGHT OF NEW YORK CITY

Over the course of the voyage, Mr. Garfield had undertaken to pay several expenses for me – both for meals and for entertainments, to which he loved to take me along. In those five days, the sum I owed him rose considerably. However, when I attempted to settle accounts with him, he nearly became indignant: "No, no!" he said. I was not to even mention it! So, I had to be content and accept his kindness.

Now, while sitting together once more in the dining room, I told him a few details of the little American's report about New York. Mr. Garfield confirmed that everything was correct. "That little student from New York has given you an excellent lesson!" he said. He added: "Soon we shall see a small part of New York – perhaps in half an hour – and then we shall slowly enter the port. It will be quite some time before we reach the spot where our ship will be moored, because it is a long way in, and the port is enormously big."

I was excited to see New York, the miraculous city of the New World, for the first time. In Paris, I had sometimes heard people speak of New York, especially about the tall buildings there – which the French people criticized, stating they spoiled the panorama. I mentioned this to Mr. Garfield. I was astonished that he did not try to defend those giant buildings of which the Americans are normally quite proud. He only said: "They are correct, in a certain sense. The French have good taste as connoisseurs of art. However, we did not build those tall buildings as an adornment for our city. We were forced out of bitter necessity, as the city has long been overpopulated. When it became absolutely necessary to expand, there was no space to the left or to the right, neither forward nor backward, on the ground. Therefore, building upward was the only way to go. As these were built of necessity more than aesthetic reasons, we constructed them to be as practical as possible."

He continued: "When you see the skyline from afar, the view may not make a favorable impression. However, if you look at each building separately, and at close range, one must admit that their construction is extremely practical. All that, you will see with your own eyes, and soon you may judge for yourself."

When lunch was over, I went to the upper deck with Mr. Garfield. We had hardly gotten there when the young American came running towards us, joyfully calling out: "New York can be seen in the far distance!"

"I am glad to hear that!" I replied, taking out my binoculars from my pocket.

The little boy pointed with his hand to the exact direction. And now I saw, for the first time, even though still far away, New York, the miraculous American city.

I cannot deny that the picture it made did not match my expectations, at first glance.

It was quite different from the many cities I had seen so far: a giant sea of houses, big and small buildings of all kinds, as far as the eye could see… but these were surrounded by what I imagined were the remnants of high walls, towering here and there over the houses, as one might see ruins from a great blaze.

I tried in vain to figure out what I was seeing. I turned towards the little American and asked him what that might be.

He answered: "Those are the skyscrapers!"

"The magnificent skyscrapers? Dear Lord! Do they really look like that?"

"Yes, Sir, they look like that when you see them from a long distance!"

I admit, I was very disappointed. The little boy noticed and tried to blot out the impression that first sight of New York had made on me. He looked at me and said, "Wait a bit, until we get nearer, so that you can see how nice they really are. Right now, we are still too far away to see them clearly."

He was right. The magnificent buildings were not yet recognizable. Seen from here, New York resembled an immensely large city of ruins! But that was only an illusion; seeing them at a closer range would be the way to notice and appreciate their true splendor.

NONNI IN AMERICA

CHAPTER 29

ENTERING THE MEGACITY NEW YORK

At last, I spotted New York! As yet, we were still on one of the promenade decks —myself, the noble Mr. Garfield and the little American boy, who considered it a matter of honor to familiarize me, the inexperienced traveler, with the splendors of New York. He quickly grabbed my hand and said: "We must climb to the highest deck at once! From there, we shall have the best view of the port and the city!"

"With much pleasure, little friend!" I answered. We left Mr. Garfield, who remained with some friends on the lower deck, and climbed the stairs to the top deck, where we made ourselves comfortable. Then, the agile little boy began explaining everything I was able to see from there. As the boat rushed forward with great speed, the view kept changing, accordingly.

On the left, a great landscape emerged before us, covered by houses too numerous to count. It seemed itself an immensely big city.

"Is that a part of New York?" I asked the boy.

"Yes," he said, "it is Richmond, which at one time was a suburb, but now is part of New York."

On the right, but still further away, another landscape appeared, also covered by many buildings.

"What is that city called?" I asked the boy.

"That is Brooklyn," he said. "It is another big city which is also part of New York, just like Richmond."

"So, the city of New York is on both sides of the water, to the left and to the right?" I asked.

"Yes, certainly," answered the boy. "Richmond and Brooklyn are the first two places you see when you approach New York from the Atlantic."

At high speed, we sailed between the two giant suburbs – Richmond and Brooklyn – and soon encountered another city behind Brooklyn.

I pointed there and said to the little boy: "There is another enormous city behind Brooklyn! It seems to be even bigger than Richmond and Brooklyn! Now, that must be the main city of New York, am I right?"

The little American answered with a smile: "Oh no, that is not yet the real New York – it is not big enough – it is what we call Queensborough, just another part of New York. The main city has not yet appeared. We shall soon be there."

I was a bit overwhelmed by the immense expansion of this city which kept unfolding itself before my eyes. I could see from above everything to the right and to the left because I was sitting on the top deck of the "Berengaria" as if on a mountaintop.

"Now we are in the outer port of New York," said the boy.

"Does that port have a special name?" I asked.

"Yes," he replied, "it is called 'The Narrows,' and it lies exactly between the two New York suburbs of Richmond and Brooklyn. We have just passed it, but now we are entering a much bigger port which stretches up to the Manhattan peninsula."

"What is that port called?"

"It is 'The Upper New York Bay'."

Now I could see in the far distance a new area approaching with an uncountable number of buildings, as big as an entire sea.

My little friend saw what I was about to ask. He said in a solemn tone: "That is, at last, New York

City proper! There it is, on a peninsula called Manhattan. On that peninsula there are the two suburbs, Manhattan and – a bit further away – The Bronx."

"The Bronx!" I cried out, "The Bronx is there? I shall be staying at a fine university there, with approximately ten thousand students, as I was told. I will be there for at least two months."

"What is the name of that university?" asked the boy.

"'Fordham University,' New York City, Bronx. That is the address."

"I know it well," my young friend said. "It is very famous!"

"The students at Fordham University are said to be the best athletes in the United States," I continued. "They win almost all their athletic competitions with the sportsmen of other cities. I was also told that the rector of Fordham

University is a Mr. Gannon, whose family is one of the most distinguished of New York."

While we were talking about all that, the "Berengaria" was nearing to the headland of Manhattan. The boy informed me that the headland lay between two rivers. One of them is rather wide and is called the Hudson River. The other one is smaller, and is called the East River. Both rivers are bridged by quite a number of splendid structures.

The nearer we got to Manhattan, the more I admired its splendor and beauty. The boy noticed my emotion and said: "Manhattan is truly the most beautiful part of New York. There are the biggest, most beautiful buildings and monuments of all the city. They also have the nicest and longest streets: there are streets nearly twenty miles long! Fifth Avenue is one of the most perfect streets of the whole world."

I have to say that I had not expected to see all that I took in. I could not help being amazed.

Suddenly, I noticed that the ship slowed and turned towards a pier. Many tugboats appeared, similar to those I had seen in Southampton. And then the difficult maneuvering began, aiming to ease the enormously huge ship into the right place at the quay. We watched these operations with interest, until the "Berengaria" was finally positioned at the bulwark of the harbor.

I could not thank the little boy enough for the great friendliness with which he explained everything to me. While discussing the last few events, the young American suddenly stopped and said: "There is one thing we have forgotten! I have not yet told you anything about the traffic in New York city. We must catch you up on that!"

Of course, that could only be done from the highest deck. After we ascended there, he looked excitedly towards the city and waited for a few moments. Then, he quickly pointed in a certain direction.

"Can you see that?" he cried out.

I looked to the indicated spot and saw a long train storming along, high above all the roofs, rattling and banging with a terrible noise.

"What sort of train is that?" I asked the boy.

"That is an Elevated, or El-Train," he replied.

"An elevated train?" I repeated. I did not understand the word. I only knew that the English word 'elevated' meant something like 'heightened' in German.

The boy explained: "That's what we call them in New York. Those trains cross the city day and night, high above the buildings. There are lots of such trains in New York," he continued. "A great number of trains also cross the city on the ground, and still more are called 'Subways,' which are the underground trains."

By and by I let my eyes wander over the city; I detected an extremely heavy traffic, especially where the 'Elevated' trains were running.

Before we parted that night, the little American praised again his favorites, the skyscrapers, and asked me with a smile: "They do look much better up close than from afar, don't they?"

I had to agree.

"And, when you visit the biggest ones, you will want to return again and again," he continued, joking.

After we had spent quite some time on the top deck, we finally headed back downstairs to prepare ourselves for the formalities regarding our landing.

CHAPTER 30

FORDHAM UNIVERSITY

As the "Berengaria" found its place in the port of New York, she came to rest amidst innumerable other ships from countries all over the world.

Many American officials began boarding. There was now commotion among the passengers because many things had to be put in order. Thousands of suitcases, boxes and crates of all kinds were carried up on deck, and everyone busily tried to keep their belongings together. As I had already gathered my complete luggage carefully in my cabin, I was able to watch the commotion in peace.

I found it fascinating to think that, in that moment, I was in the middle of the port of the New York metropolis, surrounded by the five huge "Boroughs:" Richmond, Brooklyn, Queens, Manhattan and The Bronx. I felt like a tiny atom among the millions of people living in that huge city. That thought put me into a highly peculiar mood, and that sense remained with me throughout my stay.

The various checks being conducted by the Health Commission and the passport authority did not interest me much. I used these hours of waiting to say goodbye to my travel companions, Mr. Garfield and the dear little American boy, who had been so extraordinarily friendly during the whole voyage.

The landing procedure lasted into the night. The following day, all passengers left the ship. Our luggage was taken separately by porters to an immensely big hall nearby, filled with thousands of suitcases, boxes and bags of all sorts. The passengers were guided to that hall through a narrow corridor, where they could claim and retrieve their belongings after each piece had been inspected by American officials. Due to the great number of passengers, I imagined I would have to wait for several hours in that hall… but, suddenly, Mr. Garfield approached, accompanied by a porter with my luggage – what a joyful surprise! They took me directly to the officials who were checking the luggage, and exchanged a few words with them, whereupon my suitcases were examined immediately and I was allowed through!

I could not thank Mr. Garfield enough for the extraordinary friendliness which he had shown me during the voyage across the Atlantic Ocean.

When I exited that hall, a friend from Europe, now living in New York, spied me and approached me. I had informed him by letter about my arrival. That friend was Professor Aßmuth from Fordham University.

In a true New York "cab" – as taxis are called there – Professor Aßmuth lead me through the indescribable throng of the metropolis, from the port to the Borough of The Bronx, where Fordham University was situated.

During this first drive through the streets of New York, it dawned on me that I had taken the decisive step for my world trip – I was on an entirely new continent! From here on, everything would be new and unknown.

Professor Azmuth said that a room awaited me at Fordham, and that I could stay as long as I pleased.

"Is that possible?" I asked my friend.

"Yes, certainly!" he answered, "and the rector of the university said so himself!"

"Such hospitality!" I exclaimed. "Especially towards a guest whom he does not even know!"

We rode a bit more in silence, and then after awhile, I asked Professor Aßmuth, "How many students study at Fordham University?"

"Usually between eight and ten thousand," he replied.

"And what is the name of the rector, again? It has slipped my mind."

"His name is Robert Gannon," answered my friend. Then he added: "Rector Gannon is quite an accomplished New Yorker. He has studied not only in America, but also at several European universities."

Thus professor Aßmuth informed me about various matters in my new residence.

When we reached the university campus, our cab turned off the main road into a driveway, through a broad gate, and up to such a large bucolic estate that I could hardly believe my eyes. It looked as if we had left the city completely and entered the countryside! The streets with milling crowds had disappeared into rolling, vast meadows with big trees on either side! At some distance could be seen the various splendid university buildings called "halls" by the Americans.

Puzzled, I asked my friend: "Are we still in the city?"

"Certainly", said Professor Aßmuth. "This is why that whole university property is called *rus in urbe*, which means: 'Rural land in the middle of the city.'"

Our car rolled on until we reached the beautiful university halls. We stopped in front of one of those stately buildings and got out. Then, Professor Azmuth accompanied me to Rector Gannon, who welcomed me with great kindness and cordiality. I was to feel at home at Fordham University, he said, saying I was welcome to stay as long as I wished. I thanked this extremely friendly gentleman with all my heart for his great kindness, telling him that I planned to stay about three months.

"Isn't that a bit short?" he said. "Do you think you can get to know New York, and the American experience, during that time?" Had this not been one stop on a much longer journey ahead, I may have considered his offer.

Nevertheless, I was welcomed to Fordham University, where I was put on the same level as the other inhabitants and professors – however, it seemed, I was offered all kinds of extra attention as a guest. I can barely begin to describe the effort made to make my stay at the university comfortable. One particular man who at the time also lived at Fordham, a Frenchman named Callens, nearly overwhelmed me with his favors and services alone.

And so, I stayed for three months in that small earthly paradise, from the beginning of September to the beginning of December 1936.

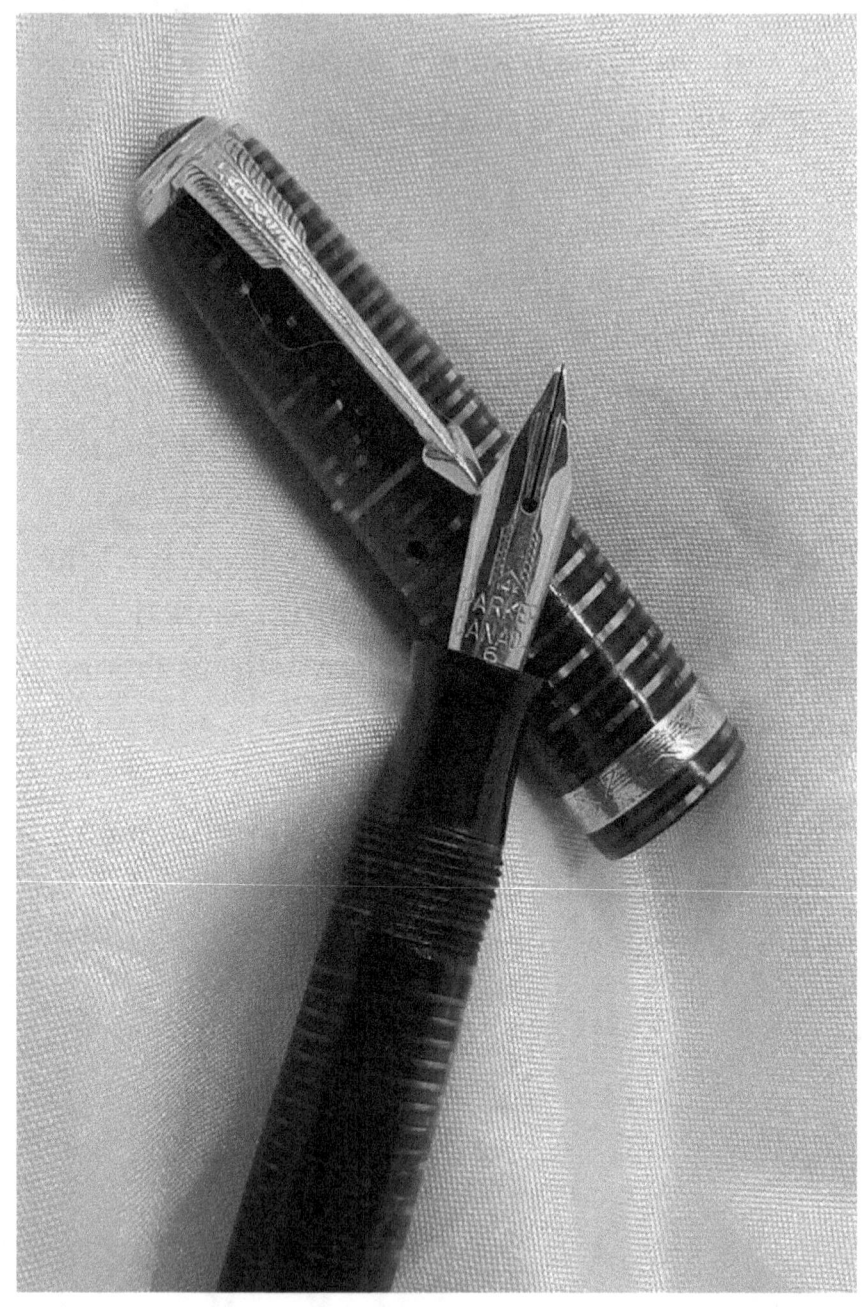

CHAPTER 31

FIRST ADVENTURES AT FORDHAM

After being welcomed by the kind-hearted rector, Mr. Gannon, another one of the professors guided me to my room. When I entered, I saw that my luggage had already arrived. But apart from that, something else gave me great pleasure: on my desk, there was a whole heap of letters … letters from Europe!

"They are probably letters from my young friends there", I said to myself. Immediately, I sat down at the table and began to examine them. I was correct: indeed, the majority of the letters came from the dear little and great friends whom I gained through the talks about my adventures as a boy on lecture tours in various European countries. But how did they know my actual address? And why did so many write to me?

Pondering that riddle, I soon recalled how many people I told that I was finally going to take the journey around the world I'd dreamed of since childhood, and that I would first stay with friends at Fordham University in New York. Thus, it was easy for them to find me.

Then I started reading the letters. Many of the young letter-writers wished they could join me on my world trip, advising me strongly to write down everything that was interesting and important. Some also cautioned that I take good care, lest wild animals devour me! Well! I had already planned to keep my eyes and ears open, and to record as many beautiful and precious things from the "Promised Land" as I could. My young and old friends in Europe were right in reminding me to pay attention to everything. They were probably thinking of the scouts in the Bible returning from the foreign lands, loaded with huge grapes and full grain. Indeed, I did hope to see the grapes in America, because at school I was taught that the grapes which thrive in Europe were initially from America. I imagined also visiting Argentina, the wheat country. But the scouts in the Bible brought home more than those few grapes and those few ears which they carried on their shoulders; more importantly, they brought their stories and descriptions home to share with everyone who welcomed them back. The many letters which I had received inspired me to strive to record and share stories from my visit to the New World. Hoping to foster love among the nations, I strove to honor the wishes of these letter-writers by recording the simple, everyday details of what I saw and heard, rather than just getting caught up in my own thoughts.

Once I read everything over, I quickly wrote some short cards in reply to a few of those kind letter-writers, telling them a few words of how happy my voyage had been so far and how well I was taken care of in New York.

Then, I decided to go out and take my first walk on my own into the big city. This would truly be my first step into a completely new life!

I kept my route brief, walking slowly through a few long streets and quietly watching the hustle and bustle in the city. It felt as if everything happening was for my pleasure. After my initial curiosity was satisfied, I withdrew from the crowd, quite content for the moment. On re-entering the house, the porter approached me saying: "While you were away, a gentleman came from the city and asked if he could talk with you."

"Who could he have been?" I asked the porter.

"I don't know," he said. "The gentleman was completely unknown to me."

"Do you think he knows me?"

"Yes, he does. He said that he met you once in Europe."

"How could he have known that I am here?" I asked.

The porter answered: "He read it in the papers."

"In the papers?"

"He said that European papers had published reports about you."

I further inquired: "Do you know his name?"

"Yes, he said his name is Fisher."

"Is he an American?"

"Yes, he is a New Yorker, and a businessman."

"And where is he now?"

"He has gone back home, but he wants to come back this afternoon."

I was rather curious, as it was impossible for me to guess who that visitor might be. Mr. Fisher? A businessman in New York who had known me in Europe? Very mysterious… I could not remember in Europe an American called Fisher! Perhaps Mr. Fisher made a mistake! In any case, I stayed in my room that afternoon.

A few hours later the porter came to me. "Mr. Fisher is here," he said. "He is waiting for you in the reception room." I went with him to one of the many parlors of the house.

I knocked on the door. "Come in!" was the answer from inside.

I opened the door. A gentleman, totally unknown to me, was seated next to the table. He got up at once and approached me, smiling kindly. We greeted each other and sat down.

The gentleman began: "You have not changed at all since we saw each other last time."

I looked at the completely strange gentleman in astonishment and said: "Pardon me, Sir… but I cannot remember ever having seen you." As I said that, an uncanny sense came over me, as if I had met that gentleman somewhere in the past, after all. But when…? And where…? I could not remember!

The gentleman kept looking at me, smiling kindly. Finally, he said: "I can very well understand that you can't remember me instantly… but, I have not forgotten you."

I was still at a loss.

However, Mr. Fisher continued, saying: "One year or so ago, you were having lunch in a dining car in Germany. Across from you sat an American. After the meal, the American noticed, to his horror that he had lost or forgotten his wallet and could not pay his bill. Immediately, you came to his aid and paid the debt."

I gradually began to remember that encounter. I grabbed the kind gentleman's hand and said: "Yes! You are right, I do remember our lunch on the German train, and I am pleased to meet you here again!"

So, there we sat, chatting for a while about our encounter in Germany. All the time, the amiable American gentleman did not stop thanking me for the small service I had rendered him a year ago. I asked him to neither think nor speak of it any longer, because what I did for him was much too unimportant. Besides, helping him in his awkward situation felt normal for me. It was a matter of the simplest tact. However, he felt my small service was something much bigger than it had been in reality. He put his hand in the pocket and took out a small package wrapped in white paper, and said: "Now you have to allow me to return the favor."

I guessed his intention and protested: "No, no! You must not do this under any circumstances…!"

But, my quest was in vain. The noble-minded, much-too-grateful Mr. Fisher removed the white paper and put the gift on the table. It was a Parker Vacumatic, by far the best and most valuable American fountain pen which existed!

There was nothing I could do about it. I had to accept this precious gift – in return for the tiny little help I had rendered my fellow traveler.

I shall never forget the noble and kindhearted Mr. Fisher. After chatting a bit longer, we parted as good friends.

CHAPTER 32

AN ENCOUNTER OUT OF THE PAST

The visit of the noble American gentleman, Mr. Fisher, was a great pleasure for me. However, it was only the first of several unexpected encounters which followed. One such instance:

From the year 1883 onwards, in my younger years over half a century earlier, I was a gymnastics teacher at a college near Copenhagen in Denmark. I held this post for many years. In the year 1912, there was a boy named August Arnold among my students. Little August was a dear, talented boy who got along with others easily. I vividly remember that he was successful in all subjects, and above all, he was a good gymnast. Hardly eleven years old, he had even mastered the so-called "Salto mortale" jump. He was a brave young man, a little knight without fear and blame. But when he was between thirteen and fourteen, he had the misfortune to quarrel with one of his teachers about some trivial matter. By the end of that week, he had bad marks in that class. His father, a very severe man, chastised him badly and threatened him with consequences if his marks did not improve by the following weekend. The poor boy tried as best he could, but his teacher gave him bad marks once again, which he knew he would have to show to his father.

On his way home, his fear and horror grew, and he could not bear to face his father. Full of despair, he fled to Copenhagen, which was five to six kilometers from his home. He went straight to the seaport and asked if there was a ship which would sail into the wide world. He was shown a boat preparing for a voyage to Australia. Quickly and resolutely, the unhappy little boy climbed on board and asked for the captain.

"Please, captain," he said, "take me with you as a shipboy!"

Strangely, the captain agreed to his plea immediately. He was accepted as a shipboy and indeed sailed into the wide world. For a long time, the college and his parents knew nothing of his whereabouts, fearing he had disappeared without a trace! Many months later, he did write to his parents after all, but he remained at sea.

Thus, over twenty years passed by! In all those years, I never heard anything from him.

But – guess what happened? On one of my first days at Fordham University, the porter came to my room and said: "You have a visitor again."

"Who is it?" I asked.

"I did not hear his name, but he wants to speak with you urgently," said the porter. "He is a New Yorker who lives only a few streets away from here. He is waiting in the reception room."

I went there immediately.

When I entered the reception room, I welcomed the visitor in English and asked him if he wanted to talk with me.

"Yes, I would love to speak with you," he answered, to my surprise, in Danish.

"Are you a Dane?" I asked.

"Yes, Sir, and I know you from Denmark, many years ago!"

Quite puzzled, I asked: "Where did we meet in Denmark?"

He answered: "Saint Andrew's College, near Copenhagen."

I was speechless as I looked at him firmly. Who might he be? I paused…

The gentleman smiled and said: "Can you really not remember me? We were good friends, after all."

I tried to remember, but in vain. Finally, I said: "I am sorry… but I confess that I cannot figure out who you are. May I ask your name?"

The mysterious visitor announced: "I am August Arnold!"

I almost fell to the ground in wonder. "Dear Lord!" I exclaimed. "Are you really my dear little student and friend August Arnold who performed the 'Salto mortale' so perfectly? Can I really believe it?"

"Yes, you can believe it, because — August Arnold, that's me!"

Imagine my amazement! There I was, standing face-to-face in front of that dear little friend who had been considered missing and lost! I embraced my student, who was not a boy anymore, but had grown into a strong man.

He wished to tell me his complete story. It was like a fascinating novel. As a shipboy, he suffered a lot. With his energy and competence, he managed to overcome all the blows of fate, and in the end, he had found a place in New York where he could live quietly and in peace. He married and became a father of several children. I promised to visit his house soon.

I spent several pleasant hours with him and his story that afternoon. It was such a treat for me to find my old student in this huge metropolis! When I set out to journey around the world, I had not imagined there would also be such peculiar (and most welcome) encounters.

I not only discovered that dear friend from bygone days, but over my stay in New York, I also had the great pleasure by and by to find other pupils whom I had taught in Denmark fifty years before. Some had become wealthy and were living lives of ease. Others, however, struggled more. All of them were equally dear to me. What pleased me most is that none were unhappy or dissatisfied, regardless of their circumstances.

One such reunion was with another extremely talented pupil whom I lectured and cared for in Denmark in the year 1884. While he was still very young, and his studies were only beginning, he was put in the lowest class, where I first met him. The school authorities entrusted him to me personally, and I took the best care of him. I looked after him not only during the school year but also during the holidays which he spent away from home. He came from a distinguished aristocratic family who excelled in civil service, not only in Denmark, but also in other countries, especially in Austria. He and I were only a few years together at the Danish college before our paths of life parted, and for many decades we did not hear from one another. When I began my world trip in 1936, my dear little "foster child" had already been past my horizon for fifty years. To that end, I did not even know where he might be in the wide world. But imagine, I was to find him again, as well, in the American megapolis! Here is how that happened: The porter at the university called on my phone. "An elderly gentleman is here," the porter told me, "and he hopes to speak with you."

I went to the reception room at once and knocked on the door.

Inside a loud voice called: "Kom ind!" That was Danish for "Come in!"

I opened the door and entered the room.

An elderly gentleman who had been sitting next to the table got up and greeted me with a smile and a light bow. I grabbed his hand, pressed it and asked him to have a seat. When we were both seated, I looked at my visitor attentively. However, I was unable to recognize in him any acquaintance from the past. I said to him: "Sir, may I ask your name?"

Smiling kindly, my guest looked at me and said: "About fifty years ago, you would not have asked for my name, because you knew it very well."

"Fifty years ago!" I repeated, ponderingly looking at my visitor.

I thought aloud: "Fifty years ago, I was a teacher at a college near Copenhagen in Denmark. Is it possible we knew each other there?"

"You are right," he said, still smiling. "We not only knew each other well, but we were also very good friends."

I continued to study the elderly gentleman but was unable to recognize any of my former students in his face.

"I am so sorry," I said finally. "I befriended all my students in that Danish college… and I cannot recall who you are."

"In that case," the stranger said, grinning, "I will help your memory. Can you remember a very young pupil who, for a while, was your only student, and whom you sometimes called 'the little philosopher' because he asked you so many questions during class concerning eternity and similar difficult matters?"

By and by it began to dawn on my memory. The gentleman continued, saying: "Can you remember taking a walk with that little boy in Copenhagen? You walked past Thorvaldsen Museum and stopped for a short while to have a closer look at the famous paintings on the outer walls of the museum. Suddenly the boy showed you the picture of one of his ancestors, who had excelled in the Austrian civil service, there among the paintings."

Suddenly I started with realization. "Are you the little baron from more than half a century ago? One of my most favorite friends, whom I cared for not only at school, but also during vacations? Why, I thought that you had gone to the other world already, because I have not heard from you since you left that Danish college!"

We sat together for a long time, as many old memories surfaced from all sides and needed refreshing. My dear little baron had become a man who had been around the world, and for many years had been a successful writer. At last, he settled in New York and lived there happily with his wife and children. His wife was the sister of the esteemed Danish novelist Karin Michaelis.

This encounter was the most pleasant one I had in the big American city. I was firmly determined to visit him in his home; unfortunately, I was prevented from doing so in the end. But please allow me to leave you with the name, address and accomplishments of that dear friend and former little foster child: Baron Joost Dahlerup, The Osborne, 205 West 57th Street, New York, NY, USA. In the well-known publication "WHO's WHO in America," you can find honorable references about Baron Joost Dahlerup. The titles of his books are listed there too. In Denmark, Baron Joost Dahlerup has been highly honored for his successful literary activity. In 1912, he was appointed "Knight of the Danebrog Order."

CHAPTER 33

THROWN INTO THE WATER

Early on, in my first days at Fordham University, I had several invitations to give lectures at high schools, colleges and similar institutions in New York. I accepted each with great pleasure, as I knew it would be a pleasant opportunity to see the city and its sights.

One day, one of the university professors came to my room and said: "I have heard that a professor from a prestigious high school in Manhattan with several hundred students will be inviting you to visit, and maybe give a few lectures. Would you be willing to accept?"

"Yes, I am willing and ready," I replied. "You need only tell me the day and the hour."

"Fine!" said the professor. "I will let them know!"

As I had a special desire to get to know Manhattan - the heart of New York, so to speak –

that invitation was extremely welcome. I waited eagerly to find out when I should go there and what they expected from me. In the meantime, I asked my friends at Fordham to tell me more about that particular school. One of the professors at Fordham knew the high school professors there. He told me: "Many hundreds of young men and women from the best families of the city attend that high school. You will be very busy there!"

"The common language is English, I suppose?" I asked.

"Yes," he said, "but French is also spoken. You may be asked to give lectures in English and in French."

Lectures in French were no problem for me, as I had spent a big part of my life in France. French had become my second mother tongue, so to speak. However, I had only lived in England for four years, and that was long ago. For that reason, the lectures in English worried me a bit, as I had lost practice with the English language. I had the idea to get one of Charles Dickens' books and read it through quickly. That proved to be a very useful exercise!

One of my Fordham friends was a guest living there to teach French. He came to my rescue in that matter too… in a very funny way, I must say.

I had informed him about my forthcoming lectures at the Manhattan high school, mentioning my difficulties with the English language.

"The best solution," he said, "is to be thrown into the water, so to speak. Only in this way can you learn how to swim. I can help you."

I did not yet know what he meant by this, but I did not think of it any further. I was to find out soon, in quite peculiar circumstances! Pretending to show me around, he invited me to go with him to a talk at one of the big lecture halls of the university. I agreed. Five minutes before the talk was to begin, he picked me up.

He had not told me that he himself was going to be the lecturer.

In the best of faith, I accompanied him to the lecture hall. My friend suggested I step up to the podium and look around, to better acquaint myself. Innocently and unsuspecting, I obeyed. Suddenly, the door opened, and a huge crowd of students entered the hall! Quite embarrassed, I tried to climb down… but, smiling, my friend hindered me. Then, he turned towards the students and said: "Today, our Icelandic visitor at Fordham will give you a little example of his narrative skills."

Completely puzzled, I realized I was being introduced to give a lecture for which I was totally unprepared! There was no escape… I had to grin and bear it, give in and endure the inevitable.

So, I surveyed the big audience. There were approximately 60 to 70 listeners, waiting impatiently for an interesting lecture by their visiting "professor" – who, at that moment, had no idea what he should tell his inquisitive and attentive audience!

After an impressive pause to consider my options, I finally began to speak.

I informed my audience about the situation – in French. The listeners paid great attention. You could have heard a pin drop!

I said: "I entered this hall in order to see what it looks like, never expecting to give a proper lecture myself! However, as your professor wishes me to speak, I shall do so with pleasure. And, as this lesson is meant to be in French, I shall use that language, as you are accustomed."

I started narrating a short story. The students remained calm and attentive. Soon, however, it seemed as if they did not understand me well. Therefore, I stopped my talk and asked the audience if they were able to understand me.

There was no answer.

The professor, seated next to me, said: "These students have not yet made enough progress in the French language to fully understand you. However, this test has been very useful for all of us, has it not? Perhaps you ought to tell your story in English, instead."

Again, I was helpless: I now had to repeat my lecture, this time in English!

I carefully explained to my patient listeners that, unfortunately, I was not very familiar with the English language, and my lecture would therefore not be very interesting. From all sides there came lively comments:

"No, no! We understand!"
"You speak English quite well!"
"Please, go on...!"

So, I pressed on, even with my weak English, until the end of the lecture. And although I knew that I made mistakes now and then, the whole audience applauded enthusiastically when I finished. From all sides they shouted that my English was not only good, but excellent, and superb! (That was of course an exaggeration, but it proved the fine character of those students. How can people in Europe say that Americans are impolite? I can assure you that I never experienced anything of the rude sort. On the contrary, I was often surprised and delighted by the fine manners and the noble sentiments of our American friends. I shall never forget how kind, friendly and polite Americans always and everywhere behaved towards me).

At the end of my lecture, the professor told the audience that he had contrived that experiment to convince me that I was able to give lectures in English. Thanking me again, the audience left the hall. On the way back to my room, the professor said kindly: "I hope you won't hold it against me that I threw you into the water. I did so to prove that you are indeed very capable to give lectures in English."

He added: "Keep in mind, after all, that we are not in Europe. We are not meticulous about a foreigner speaking our language. We can handle your mistakes. I heartily endorse your giving lectures, at Manhattan high school and elsewhere, in English, by all means. You have nothing to fear; your mistakes are too minor to bring you harm."

Thus, I was deemed capable to give lectures in English to my American audiences.
You can imagine how happy I was! That unique American spirit of encouragement profoundly helped me to conquer my speech anxiety, and freed me from any such fear going forward.

NONNI IN AMERICA

CHAPTER 34

LECTURES IN MANHATTAN

A few days after my practice lecture at Fordham University, I received the official invitation by the school authorities of Manhattanville College. I would go there the next day and give a lecture to the whole college – in English.

I accepted and immediately began preparing.

The next day I took an "El" train – the "elevated" railway, which took me amazingly fast from The Bronx to Manhattan, high above the roofs of the houses. Along the way I admired the magnificent, long streets of that part of New York.

I was welcomed with extraordinary kindness and true American politeness. In the afternoon I gave my lecture in English to the all-girl student body in their great assembly hall. The students were exemplary and made the best impression on me. When I left late in the afternoon, the lady principal accompanied me to a car which she had ordered for me and which was already waiting. As we parted, she surprised me by saying: "We all are very grateful for your kind visit and for your lecture. It would be a great pleasure for us if you could come again… not only for a few hours like today, but perhaps an entire week. You could find some rest here with us, and maybe we could ask you to give a few more lectures?"

I accepted her invitation with pleasure, promising to give all the lectures she wished. The principal was grateful. Later, she mentioned that some of the young lady students hoped for a lecture in French. I was delighted. The date of my week-long stay was decided as my first visit concluded.

Immediately on returning to Fordham, I went to the professor (the same man who played the funny trick on me in his lecture hall) and told him how my visit to Manhattanville College, along with my lectures in English, had gone.
"There! You see!" he said, "How true is the proverb: *'In order to learn how to swim, one has to be thrown into the water.'* In my lecture hall, I threw you

into the water – and now you can swim without any difficulty."

That kind American professor was right: English lectures were no longer difficult for me. Invitations for new lectures also did not take long in coming. On the contrary, they came from many sides and in great number. Thus, I had the pleasure to connect with people all over New York as well as outside of the city. Once, I even accepted an invitation to spend a whole week in the nearby beautiful and rich state of Pennsylvania, with its splendid countryside. I was received and treated with the greatest friendliness everywhere I went.

I was to return to Manhattanville after my stay in Pennsylvania. I proceeded there immediately and enjoyed my days in that fine institution. I also gave several lectures: some in English, others in French. However, that week felt more to me like rest than work.

Manhattanville college is situated in the middle of a beautiful park, through which I had permission to walk daily. In front of the main building there was a big square. From morning till late afternoon, a great number of elegant cars pulled up and stopped there. I asked one of the students about those cars, and she answered that those were the cars of the students who live off-campus. "They drive here every morning," she said, "and in the afternoon, they return home."

"Does every student have her own car?" I asked.

"Oh, yes. At least, most of them do," she replied.

I considered with amazement how many cars there are in America. Almost everybody can drive a car - not only men, but also women, and even young girls! I thanked the young student and walked further into that gorgeous park. There, I was about to have a sweet little adventure – which, being an animal lover, I enjoyed greatly.

A little boy of about twelve approached me, greeting me politely: "I beg your pardon, Sir! Have you seen the squirrels living here in the park?"

I answered that, so far, I had not yet noticed any squirrels. "Are there many squirrels living here in the park?" I asked him.

"Oh, yes, Sir", he said. "And if you have nuts to give them, they become very trusting."

"Where could I get any nuts here?" I asked.

"I shall bring you some in a minute!" he said.

Saying this, he ran into a house and returned shortly afterwards with a handful of small nuts, which he handed to me with a smile. I thanked him for his friendliness and put the nuts into my pocket. Then I made my way to the next garden path between the tall trees. I looked around all sides but did not discover any squirrels.

After about ten minutes, I suddenly spied one sitting on a branch in the treetop. I took a nut out of my pocket and showed it to the cute little creature. When I saw that it noticed the nut, I sat down on a bench nearby. The small animal began climbing down the trunk of the tree. When it reached the ground, it approached me… and I remained on the bench without stirring.

The squirrel reached my bench, and, without the least sign of fear, it stopped right in front of me, gazing quietly. I looked back at him, trying to muster my friendliest face possible, to gain the little creature's trust. A few minutes passed. Then, the squirrel made a quick movement, looking to the side. I threw a glance in that direction, and with pleasure, discovered a second squirrel! Hopping cautiously over the garden path, it came nearer. It did not take long before that squirrel stopped beside the other one, turning round to look at me firmly, exactly like the other one.
I remained calmly where I was, observing the cute little creatures.

All three of us stayed still. After a few minutes, I put a hand in my pocket and took out a nut. I held it between two fingers in my right hand and showed it to both little friends without saying a word. They gazed incessantly at the small nut between my fingers without moving whatsoever. Slowly, I put my other hand in my pocket and took out a second nut… showing both nuts to the squirrels.

They stayed immobile but seemed to devour the nuts with their eyes. I offered both nuts very slowly and at the same time to the two little animals.

Immediately, they hopped to my knee and helped themselves to the nuts! Then, both turned around, jumped to the ground, and ran quickly to the nearby meadow. Each dug a hole, put its nut into the hole, and covered the hole with soil, pressing it tightly with their little front paws.

When they finished, they ran back to me quickly, sitting down on the path next to each other exactly as before, looking at me firmly in the same manner.

After a few moments, I took again two nuts out of the pocket. This time, however, I put them in the buttonhole of my coat. Then I crossed my arms and waited.

At once, both little friends jumped upon my knees and, with great skill, removed its nut from the buttonhole, jumped down, ran to the meadow and buried the nut in the ground as before. Then, a few jumps back …and both sat again, in front of me on the path, waiting expectantly.

Again, I took two nuts out of my pocket, showed them to the dear little animals, and this time put them into my coat pockets – one in the right pocket, the other one in the left pocket. I crossed my arms and sat still. A few moments later both animals jumped upon the bench, one to my right, the other one to my left, put their small front paws in my half-open coat pockets, fetched the nuts and ran to the meadow, burying them like the others. Just as quickly, they bounded back to me and sat down on the path again.

Now I put two nuts in my hand, showed them to both squirrels, closed my hand and waited. Immediately both creatures jumped to my knees again and gazed firmly at my closed right hand.

I never expected one of the squirrels to strike my hand with the sharp claws of his right front paw! He left a small, bleeding wound, but I could not hold it against the little animal. I gave each another nut, and both accepted their small present with pleasure on the path next to my feet. This time, they cracked the hard shells skillfully and enjoyed the kernels right there.

When I got up to go home, both squirrels - who had become almost tame by then - followed me like two little doggies to the entrance of the house.

There, we parted as good friends.

NONNI IN AMERICA

CHAPTER 35

A VISIT TO THE WOOLWORTH AND EMPIRE STATE BUILDINGS

One day when I was sitting in my peaceful room in Fordham University there was a sudden knock on my door.

I called: "Come in!"

The door opened and a young university student named Hubert entered. I knew him well, and his parents and I had met several times.

"It is a pleasure seeing you, dear Hubert." I said to the young student, offering him a chair.

Sitting down, he said: "My mother wonders if you would like to visit the two highest New York skyscrapers today. We talked of them during your last visit, the Woolworth and Empire State buildings, if you recall."

"Your mother is so kind to invite me!"

"Oh, don't mention it!" smiled Hubert. "We agreed to go with you, after all, and it would be my pleasure to accompany you. So, if you are free today and would like a look at the two skyscrapers, I will gladly take you."

A few days earlier, at his parents' home, we talked much about New York's skyscrapers. I told them some of the information the little American boy on the "Berengaria" had given me, and they kindly offered Hubert as a guide, should I wish to see them up close. Now, he was here.

I thought about it for a moment, then said: "Very well, it suits me perfectly! Let us be on our way!" I asked Hubert to wait a few moments while I got ready, and then we went by car into the indescribably crowded heart of New York.

On the way, I asked my young guide: "Which of the two skyscrapers should we visit first: the Empire State Building, or Woolworth?"

"I would prefer to visit Woolworth first," replied Hubert. "Thus, we would begin with the smaller one and later proceed to the bigger. That might be more interesting, because the second building will be even more spectacular than the first."

"You are right, Hubert," I answered. "That is true."

After a short pause I asked the good boy: "Have you often been in the Woolworth building?"

"Very often," he said, "Fordham University has rented a few floors in the Woolworth building for approximately three thousand students because the campus itself does not have enough space. That means a part of our university is located in the Woolworth building."

"How is that possible?" I exclaimed. "Are there really lectures for our students held in the Woolworth building?"

"Yes, for three thousand Fordham students."

Realizing he knew a great deal about the wonderful Woolworth building, I took the opportunity to ask him many questions:

"Do you know how tall the Woolworth building is, exactly?" I asked him.

"It is 792 feet high, that is, 240 meters. Before the Empire State Building came to be, the Woolworth was the tallest building on earth. As you know, the Empire State Building is now much taller than that. Nevertheless, Woolworth is regarded a miracle among the skyscrapers of New York."

"Two hundred and forty meters high!" I gasped. "To us Europeans, that seems unbelievable! Even our highest towers are nothing compared with the height of such buildings!"

Hubert smiled and said: "Yes, I know… That's why Americans are a bit proud of our skyscrapers."

"That is understandable," I replied. "When was the Woolworth building finished?"

"It was finished in 1913, in a very remarkable way."

"Can you tell me about it?"

"I will try," began Hubert. "It was on the 24th of April, 1913. The United States Congress gathered with President Wilson in the White House in Washington. Precisely at midnight, President Wilson pressed a button, and eighty thousand bulbs began to glow brightly in the Woolworth building in New York. Thus, the building was opened!"

"How wonderful!" I exclaimed.

"Yes, and it is still a splendid spectacle each time all the lights are on," added the young student.

"Did you really say eighty *thousand* electrical lights? Does the building have that many lights? Could you be mistaken?"

"It is absolutely true. The Woolworth building still has eighty thousand electrical lamps. And when all of them are lit, the building seems to stand in a sea of lights!"

"Amazing…" I mused. Then, I continued: "What about the elevators, or lifts. in the Woolworth building? I suppose there must be many of them, since so many people are coming and going, up and down, in such a huge building."

"I cannot say precisely how many elevators there are in the Woolworth building," said the young student, "but, to give you an idea, thirty-five thousand people use the elevators in that building every day. They are operated by a great number of young people dressed in uniform."

Among other things, Hubert also told me that the Woolworth building had two thousand and four hundred telephones, through which approximately thirty-eight thousand telephone calls were made daily. I followed his explanations attentively, asking questions from time to time, such as: "How is it that this incredibly high and heavy building does not sink into the ground? The weight of such a giant building must be enormous!"

"True," he said. "That was one of the most important considerations when constructing the building. It was solved by laying a foundation of stone lowered one hundred and ninety feet into the ground. Beneath that is the existing bedrock. The heavy foundation stones sit on that rock, and then on top sits the huge building. Expert architects say that such a building could not have been constructed if that bedrock were not already there. In fact, all of the skyscrapers of New York sit on such a foundation."

"There must be many people living in that building. Do you know how many?"

"Yes, I know," replied the young Fordham student. "Approximately fourteen thousand."

Suddenly my young guide looked up and announced: "We are almost there. We can get out here so that we only have to walk a very short way to the entrance of the building."

I looked outside quickly. However, one could not see anything but a busy street stretching far into the distance. It was a hustle and bustle of people and all makes of cars, with rows of buildings on each side of the street, such as you can see in all major cities. However, looking upward startled me… for, what did I see? High above in the clouds there was an enormous light grey mass, strong and firm. Amazed, I pointed upwards. Hubert looked up … and said, laughingly: "That is your first glimpse of the Woolworth building! At first, you can only see the top above the roofs of all the other buildings. But in a few minutes we will be there, directly in front of Woolworth."

I looked out at the street once again. The normal buildings stood there in line … but above them, high in the clouds, I saw again that wall of grey. It was so new … so unusual… that I could not take my eyes from that compact mass in the middle of the clouds! It was so new … so unlikely … so fantastic … that I was speechless for the moment.

Slowly I came to myself again.

In that moment, the expression for such buildings in Europe began to make sense: sky<u>scraper</u> … *gratte-ciel.* Yes, that wonderful building truly seemed to pierce the clouds!

"I see we can drive almost up to the entrance of the Woolworth building after all," said Hubert, correcting his earlier opinion and altering course slightly. A few minutes later the car turned toward the lower row of buildings and stopped in front of that miracle of the world which we wanted to visit.

The huge Woolworth building stood there, in front of us — that wonder of human craftmanship and initiative!

I got out and stood beside the car, spellbound. What I saw could not be compared with anything I knew. It was completely incomprehensible for me that people should build such high buildings and want to live in the clouds. I imagined the seagulls of Iceland with thousands of nesting places high up on the steep rocky walls, but I just could not understand how people could live in the clouds amidst a confusing array of peepholes.

Then Hubert came around, jolting me out of my dreams and summoning me to go with him to the main entrance of that splendid building. The entry was like a huge portal, forged by the best material. We entered into a hall itself as high as a tower, where gold and silver and precious marble were displayed in abundance.

It was like being in a magic castle. I had seen grand palaces before, but hardly greater splendor anywhere!

My amazement about everything I encountered here was partly due to the assumptions I'd made about American skyscrapers. I imagined these structures would be very sober and cold, constructed for architectural utility with little concern for beauty. I immediately found the opposite was true: beauty had priority, and useful matters took the back seat. As I saw more and more of the New World, I realized that neither usefulness nor beauty are compromised in these grand constructions. On the contrary, Americans seem to take great pains to make practical things as pleasing as possible; that is to say, they do not give up until the useful things are pretty, too.

I noticed the Woolworth building is constructed in Gothic style. After traversing the beautiful entrance hall, we approached the elevators. Hubert, bursting with pride for his country and its accomplishments, wanted to take me immediately to the top floor.

Our elevator car was very spacious. It looked like an elegant room! There was a good dozen passengers, both ladies and gentlemen. Our operator was an elegantly dressed young man. His uniform went very well with the splendor of his elevator.

When entering, I noticed that all gentlemen took off their hats, keeping them in their hands. I asked one of the gentlemen standing next to me why the male passengers removed their headpieces.

"We do that always when ladies are among us," he said. "We Americans respect and honor women."

When the elevator was full, our operator gave the sign for departure and our small group of people went up with enormous speed. At the top station, the elevator door opened and we entered a big, round room.

The décor was tasteful and enticing. Several doors led outside. We opened one and went out into the fresh air. The sight was indescribably wonderful. All of New York was at our feet – a limitless sea of buildings beneath us, and behind it we could see the seaport with countless ships.

Hubert pointed out several sights.

After taking in the splendid panorama for a long while, we came in and made our descent. The elevator took us from the clouds back down to the earth in a few seconds. After all, this visit was only meant to be a first acquaintance with the splendid building. Hubert planned a more proper, thorough visit for a later date. This brief introduction was to be the frame for our next visit! We left the gorgeous skyscraper and got into our car again, now to drive to the Empire State Building – the highest building on earth. Our visit there would also be a very short preparation for a longer sightseeing tour another day.

During our ride we chatted eagerly about both huge buildings. Hubert confirmed my guess that the greatest effort had been invested in rendering everything in the Woolworth building meticulously true to the original Gothic style. I was preoccupied by the idea of how the builder chose the Gothic style for Woolworth. He even named his building: "The Woolworth Cathedral" or "The Cathedral of Commerce" – as Hubert told me proudly.

"Indeed," I answered, "if I had heard it called 'The Woolworth Cathedral' or 'The Cathedral of Commerce' without having seen the building itself, I might have been shocked. But now I have seen how closely utility and beauty are related in the American mind. Therefore, I can very well imagine that, for the American, this world and the next are as closely related as religious matters are interconnected with worldly affairs. In fact, the Woolworth building consists of a very high tower reminiscent of medieval gothic with a corresponding extension, and when entering the splendid rooms one does have the feeling being in sacred halls, somehow. And, why should working places and living places not be sacred? These, too, are places for the children of God, for whom nothing can be good enough!"

It was impossible for me not to see God's loving eye and guiding hand behind that huge city through which we drove, and even in the hustle and bustle. Otherwise, what would be the purpose for all this splendor? According to His own words, "no hair will fall from our head, nor a tile from our roof, without the Father knowing and willing it." I trust that those huge buildings and masses of people also rest in His hands. The higher the buildings rise, and the larger the masses grow, the closer will be God's mercy.

Christ did not weep in vain when he saw beautifully built Jerusalem. And, not in vain "did he have compassion when he saw the great mass of people at Lake Genesareth" – as Evangelist Mark reported.

As Hubert listened, he commented partly to himself and partly to me: "I don't know that Mr. Woolworth was thinking of all those things while building his house. The Americans act more by instinct than lengthy consideration, I think."

"I might have thought that, too, before I met the Americans personally and before I saw the Woolworth building," I had to admit. "I had the idea that a kind of calculating rationality would dominate the minds in a nation which stands in the centre of world affairs. But I am coming to discover the heart and soul of the American way, which the American 'does not wear on his sleeves,' as we say in Europe. Nor is the ultimate success what we want to achieve important – but what God makes of our efforts," I continued. "That also holds true for these skyscrapers!"

Hubert did not give any answer. Instead, his concentration was on driving. And then, the car came to a halt in front of the Empire State Building.

I could see that this building had been erected with the greatest care, too. Here, however, it seemed to me that the builder's main concern was its height. Indeed, they succeeded in constructing this building one hundred and forty meters higher than the Woolworth Building. While that is – as mentioned before – two hundred and forty meters high, the Empire State Building is three hundred and eighty meters high. The Woolworth Building has sixty floors, whereas the Empire State Building has one hundred and two floors, and each floor is eleven feet high! The whole building is more than three times as high as the towers of the cathedrals of Cologne, Straßburg, Freiburg and Ulm.

The weather was fine as Hubert and I approached the front of that building. There were only some small clouds in the sky. The top of the Empire State Building hovered up so high that I could not see the topmost floors.

"When you have never seen such a tall building," Hubert said to me, "you cannot possibly imagine such height."

That I had to admit. Although I had been somehow prepared for the visit of the Woolworth Building, i.e. for the sight of a skyscraper, I was completely stunned to behold the Empire State Building. The two hundred and forty meters of the Woolworth Building led me to imagine that its topmost windows were small peepholes to the firmament; now, this façade of three hundred and eighty meters looked like a giant ladder which disappeared into the sky.

When we left the car and went inside, we soon found many people by the elevators. Those coming down from the top floors swarmed to the exit and left the building. An equally great flow of people was coming inside, like us.

Everything was furbished practically in the same manner as the Woolworth Building.

NONNI IN AMERICA

We entered one of the elevators. Several ladies and gentlemen had already boarded.
Showing politeness towards the ladies, we took off our hats, as I now knew was American custom.

A diligent American girl in a pretty uniform was the operator. She pressed a button, and the little "salon" went up immediately. We rose quickly, but it took longer than in the Woolworth Building. The elevator stopped and we got off. Although we were still inside the building, there was much space in every direction. We lingered there for a while to have a look at the splendid furnishings. There was a uniformed attendant nearby, ready to be of assistance.

Everything was exceptionally clean: no dust anywhere, and all metal pieces gleamed as if freshly polished. After looking around a bit, we discovered a door with the English sign "EXIT" meaning "This way out into the open!"

We stepped outside and stood under the open sky. It was a spacious area from which we had a splendid view over the megacity of New York. Fortunately, all remaining clouds had disappeared. The weather was clear and sunny.

The city panorama of New York made a stronger impression on me here because this location was much higher and more convenient for city viewing than the one earlier at the Woolworth Building.

After we looked around for a while, we went back to the elevators. We entered a "through train" – an elevator operating the complete journey down with no stops. More passengers joined us. Finally, the journey began, this time downwards. It went quick as lightning… a buzzing and trembling for a few seconds, then a sudden stop at the ground. We got off and exited to the street, and back to our car.

This was a most unforgettable day! I had seen the two tallest buildings of the world, and thus had experienced two world miracles! As before, this time was only meant to be a short introduction, with longer visits to follow. In fact, just a few days later, one of those longer visits took place with another good friend named Callens. However, for the time being, I had plenty of material to ponder and write about. My eyes were brimming, and my heart, too.

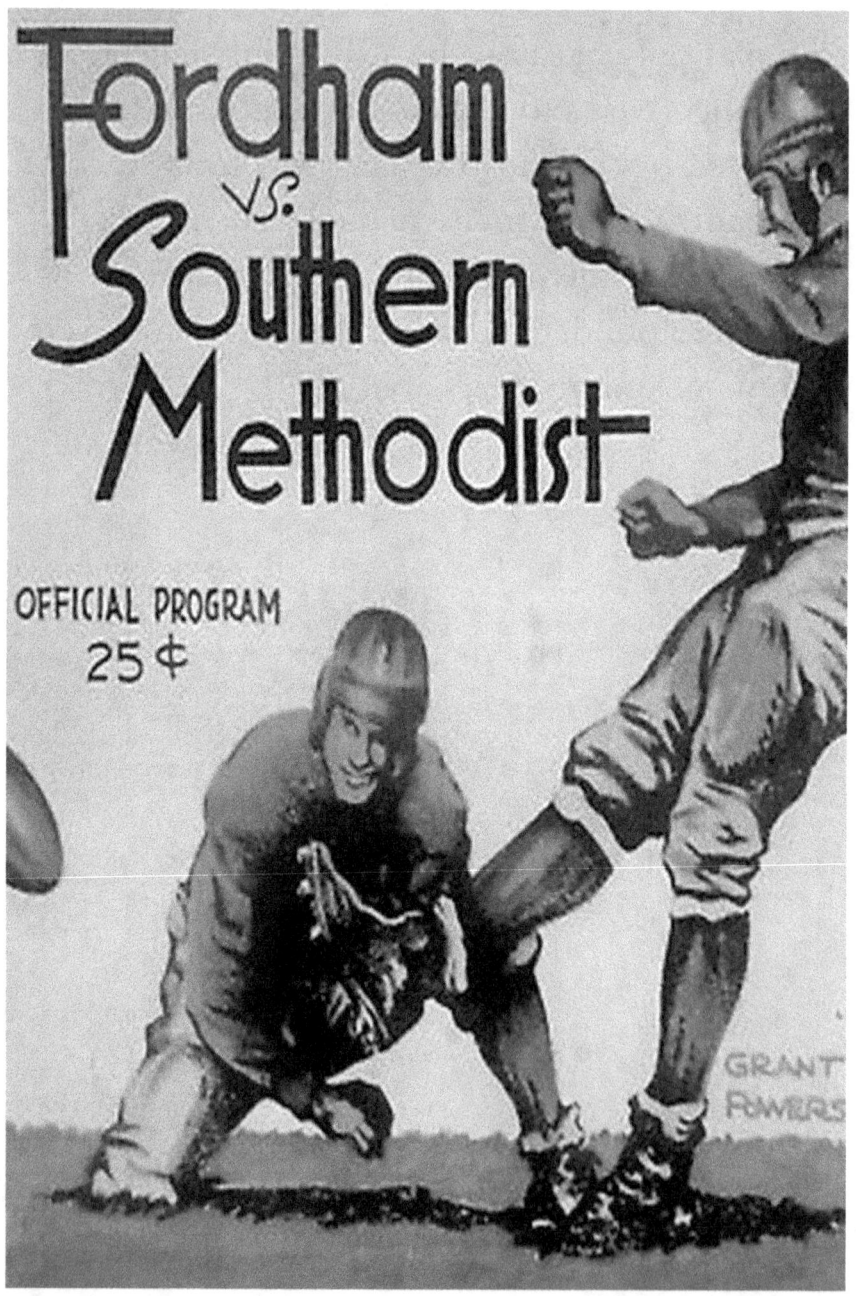

CHAPTER 36

FORDHAM VERSUS SMU

A few days after my sightseeing tour of the skyscrapers of New York, I had another very pleasant visitor to my room at Fordham University, this time a young man whom I'd met only briefly before.

He greeted me politely. I welcomed him warmly, asking him to have a seat.

Sitting down, he said: "Will you be going to the game at the stadium tomorrow against the Texas team, which begins at half past two?"

"What kind of contest is it?" I asked.

"Have you not heard about the big football game between Southern Methodist University of Texas, which is near the Gulf of Mexico, and our Fordham University team?"

"No, so far I have not heard anything about it."

"Have you really not heard anything?" he asked, pulling a newspaper out of his pocket and unfolding it. He pointed to an article on the first page. I put on my glasses and quickly perused the notice, which now interested me quite a bit.

All was indeed printed there, word by word. The next day, Saturday, 10th October 1936, was to be a showdown between the best athletes of Texas Southern Methodist University and those of our Fordham University students in an American football match. The battle was to take place in a huge stadium in New York with a capacity of more than one hundred thousand spectators. It would be a thrilling match between two important and well-known universities of the United States of America!

"That game will be a sensation," said the young student, "for Fordham University's football team has thus far been undefeated. Our athletes are considered the best in the whole country. For that reason, Fordham University often competes in big games like this. Our team has not yet lost a single match. Tomorrow's game will be hot because each side is eager to win. I strongly encourage you to go!"

"Yes, I see," I replied. "That game will be most interesting."

"I thought so," said the friendly student. And he added: "You won't regret going. I'll say it again: this match is extremely important. Our players will give it their best effort, because the visiting team has a great reputation for winning. Like our Fordham team, they are largely undefeated. The last time they played us was four years ago, when Fordham won 14-0. Now, Southern Methodist is out for revenge. They have traveled several days and nights to get here."

"All the more interesting, then, will this match be," I remarked.

"Oh yes," added my friendly visitor. "That's why we all plan on being there – not only the university students, but also the professors. I hope that our rector will go, too."

"I would not be surprised," I replied, "because it is well known that in America there is a much greater interest in sports than we have in Europe."

"That's true," said my young friend, "and we are also criticized and rebuked by Europeans for neglecting sciences in schools in favor of sports."

"That is true unfortunately; I cannot deny I've heard such remarks. But, given all that I have seen on my visit, this criticism is largely unfounded."

"I agree, it is greatly exaggerated," answered the young man eagerly. "The sciences have priority in all of our universities. But that is no reason to neglect sports. Europeans do well to put sciences first, but they ought not to forget the importance of physical exercise and sports, in our opinion."

"I am completely with you," I answered.

My friend took a freshly printed illustrated magazine out of his pocket and showed it to me.

He said: "This is the official program for tomorrow's game. You will find several pictures of the athletes of both teams who will be competing tomorrow."

I took a close look at this program. It was printed on strong glossy paper and comprised about twenty pages. Pictures of athletes from both teams were meticulously arrayed. Such muscular bodies I had hardly seen in my life. There was also a list of each team's previous matches and victories. The first page showed the title in very big letters:

FORDHAM

vs.

SOUTHERN METHODIST

Official Program

I asked the young student what "Southern Methodist" meant.

"I do know who the Methodists are," I clarified. "You can find them in all countries. They strive for the holiness of people by preaching the Gospel. However, I have never heard anything about 'Southern' Methodists."

He answered: "The Texan athletes are all Methodists, and, as they live and worship in the American south, they refer to themselves as 'Southern Methodists'."

Apparently, these young Americans regard religion and sports as closely together as the skyscraper and the cathedral.

"How extraordinarily strong and healthy these young Americans look!" I said to my visitor after regarding the pictures in the program for a while.

"Surely," he answered, "they all do train as athletes, after all."

"Athletes… Tell me, what do Americans mean by this term? In Europe, I believe that word is used in quite a different sense."

The young man answered: "We consider 'athletes' to be the strongest and best among those who try out and qualify for teams to represent American universities and other important institutions. As you know, we have a lot of sports here. But only the strongest and most robust are chosen to be on the teams which compete in the big matches to show off their training and athletic skills. Universities recruit athletes by offering great incentives and facilities. The main benefit is that these student athletes live and study in those big institutions free of charge. So, if an extraordinarily strong young person wants to attend university or college, he might be admitted free of charge."

"How so? Are you to mean that tuition, meals, room and board are granted free of charge to those young athletes during their entire academic years?"

"Yes, in such cases, all that is completely free. I shall explain it to you," continued my visitor. "American universities and colleges benefit from this system because those athletes take upon themselves the important responsibility to earn the institutions not only prestige but also a lot of money from these matches. Many times, universities earn more from sports games than they spend providing their athletes a free education."

"What are the athletes expected to do?"

"Those athletes need to be strong and ready to play in matches with other universities, and to make winning the games their priority."
"How, then, do the universities earn money enough to cover their educational costs?"

"These matches take place in the big stadiums, where there can be more than one hundred thousand spectators. Each admission ticket costs several dollars, which then yields a large stream of revenue to the university or college. The athletes themselves do not get anything from that money. They have already received their payment in the form of free tuition, board and lodging during their complete academic years."

"Which team do you think will win: our Fordham athletes, or the Southern Methodists?" I asked my student-friend.

"We are certain Fordham will win," he said. "After all, they are known as the best team."

"That is also my belief," I added.

He added: "However, I will feel sorry for Southern Methodist if they lose, because they traveled all the way from Texas, which is a journey of several days and nights."

After that, the young student got up and bade me farewell.

"Thank you very much," I said, "for your kind visit and for all the interesting information you gave me."

"Can I be sure that you will be at the stadium tomorrow to see the game?" he asked as he left the room.

I said "yes," because now I was completely determined to witness such an important event. I wondered how I could secure a favorable seat in that huge stadium. I was most interested to see how the match between these bold Texas athletes and the apparently invincible Fordham heroes would end.

NONNI IN AMERICA

NONNI IN AMERICA

CHAPTER 37

GOING TO THE BIG GAME

The match between the Texas athletes and the Fordham team was scheduled for Saturday, the 10th of October.

I set out to get a seat in the big stadium where, for almost three hours, the players would go head-to-head. It mattered to all of us in a special way: after all, our own Fordham University athletes were to play against an athletic force who had come from far away with a burning desire to win! It would be a showdown between American athletes from the north and from the south, both teams highly skilled. There were no lectures that whole morning, even though the game was not to start until half past two.

By chance, one day before the match, several important guests had arrived at Fordham University from world famous universities in Rome... erudite professors of philosophy and theology, headed by the Rector Magnificus, the

General Director of the University of Rome. All these gentlemen were invited by the American professors to attend the football game as well. Even these most distinguished Roman guests adapted easily to these peculiarly American customs. All went to the stadium together with the professors of Fordham University in a couple of cars which had been put at their disposal.

I had the honor to ride in one of those cars myself, with one of the Roman professors. For half an hour, we drove through the rolling hustle and bustle of New York until we reached the huge amphitheater – that is to say, "the stadium." We did not discuss theological questions during our ride because neither the atmosphere nor the ambience was suitable.

The Roman gentleman sitting next to me had never been in America before. He seemed to feel kind of muzzy in the unusual and unfamiliar surroundings. When we turned onto one of the most frequented streets, he cried out, completely amazed: "What a lot of people! Is there anything special going on?"

"No, nothing special is going on. It is always like that," I said.

"Amazing!" he cried out once more. "I did not think this much traffic was possible!"

"In the beginning, I was also amazed at the amount of traffic," I replied. "But soon, one gets used to it."

"Are you a New Yorker?" he asked me.

"Oh no, I am an Icelander."

"An Icelander!" he exclaimed. "How did you get here?"

"I have come here from England, and I am going to stay in the United States for a few months."

"And where will you go from here?"

"From here I shall travel to Japan, China and India, then back to Europe."

"That means you are making a circumnavigation!"

I smiled. "Yes, if you want to give it that name."

"Is that perhaps a bet?" he wondered.

"Oh no, not at all! I am simply eager to get to know God's beautiful and vast world. He has created it especially for us, after all. Later, I will share with others whatever I see and experience. I intend to write a book about my journey around the world."

I did not want the questions of this very learned and amiable Roman gentleman to lead to discussing my previous Nonni books, and so I tried to steer the conversation in a different direction by asking: "Professor, maybe it's you who is on a trip around the world?" He replied: "Oh no, not at all. I am only spending my vacation in New York. I shall stay here for a short while. Then I shall go back to Rome."

Once we reached the stadium, I helped my distinguished friend out of the car, then walked with him toward the other guests who had arrived before us with a few other Fordham professors. Now we all waited to get into the stadium and be seated. That was easier said than done, because the crowd of people pressing in on the entrance was huge. One could do little else but swim forward with the enormous swell of spectators like a rolling sea of people. And, those living floods kept rolling forward – you did not know how – nor on which path, or where to – with no individual ability to move in any other direction.

Suddenly, the immense flood seemed to rise upwards, without my knowing how or why… one wave rising after the other, thanks to the broad stairs under our feet. When our upward climb stopped, we poured forth onto flat ground. Here, we had a better view of our surroundings. I looked around and saw a lot of broad doorways.

The stream rolled forward once more, heading towards the entrances and dividing itself by them, gushing finally into the enormously vast arena.

Inside were uncountable people, one row behind the other, with each new row a little higher, like giant stairs stretching endlessly round the vast arena. The image of the antique Colosseum in Rome flashed in my mind! What a picture: a bustle of thousands upon thousands of people, restlessly moving and loudly speaking with each other, whose last rows could hardly be recognized.

We looked for a seat and sat down. It felt as if the enormous crowd might devour us! Then, I glanced upwards and could not believe my eyes. Was there really no roof? Indeed, the sky spread wide over our heads… and below on the earth was a firm, vast, flat ground. It appeared as a beautiful green meadow with firm, sandy patches. This is where the fierce match of the well-trained American athletes would be carried out.

The game was set to begin soon. Many people were talking, many were laughing, many were shouting to each other – some in a low voice, others loudly. One could not discern any words among the laughter or the shouts. The space was too vast! The mingling of the sounds – both loud and faint – reminded me of the rustling wind on a summer night.

I startled abruptly at a sudden strong, metallic sound from down below. A robust military band began to play, and all heads turned towards the direction of the music. From the crowd there was now complete silence. What a picture that band made marching in! The sounds of the horns grew stronger. Suddenly, the athletes appeared in their colorful uniforms! One team entered from the left onto the field, the other team from the right, and the teams met in the middle. They greeted each other, calmly, self-assured, elegant and proper, suggesting a certain solemnity. Then, they parted once more… and the fight began!

CHAPTER 38

CONVERSATION WITH AN ATHLETE

I must admit: Being a European inexperienced with American football makes it impossible for me to describe that game in proper detail. Everything happened incredibly fast. And everything was completely different from what I had ever seen back home.

Each tall, broad-shouldered young man was clad in long, leathery trousers tugged into colorful sports socks; club sweater on top; and soccer shoes with cleats. Most strange of all were the objects they wore on their heads! It took me several minutes to realize these were, in fact, crash helmets, just like the ones our motorcyclists might wear during their big races. I could not imagine what on earth those helmets had to do with a football match! As the teams beneath us marched to the center of the field, I saw that they were also wearing shields beneath their sweaters and trousers, giving them a strangely smooth and stiff appearance.

Whatever were they expecting to take place? Even for a European used to sports, this was a strange and unusual picture!

Then I noticed something else, which I found rather funny: the southern team from Texas carried along a little pony! It was a bit frightened and reluctant to follow. The players dragged and pulled as best they could. The pony was their mascot, their "good-luck charm," and the team's nickname was "The Mustangs" – named after the wild stallions on which Old Shatterhand and Winnetou had ridden so often. They draped a blanket over their mustang-pony in their team colors of red and white.

When Fordham's team passed by, I noticed something even stranger: These athletes, themselves clad in reddish-brown, escorted in a real, reddish-brown billy goat! Such a thing is completely unknown in Europe! I learned their nickname was "The Rams." So, it was to be a fight between the "Mustangs" and the "Rams" – or, one could say, the wild stallions against the billy goats!

I had no idea what to expect.

After the teams marched in from both left and right towards the center of the vast field, sides were chosen and the referees announced. Then a whistle, and the players took their positions.

American football consists of eleven players just like European football, but the positions of the players are completely different: the Americans use linemen, receivers, half-backs and fullbacks, along with the quarterback. They distribute seven men as strikers, one half-back each on the right and on the left, along with two "backs," i.e. defense players. Also, the goal is different from the one in Europe: it is about 5.5 meters broad and about 3 meters high. The side bars can be up to 3.5 meters longer.

And, to my bewilderment, the ball looked like an enormously big egg!

Everything was quite different, indeed!

If you have ever heard or seen anything about rugby matches, you will find great similarity between that and American football. However, in rugby there are 15 players and they do not wear protective gear, nor do they wear crash helmets on their heads like the Americans.

The match in the big stadium was not as calm as I am reporting it to you. It was impossible for me to figure out everything because one action followed the next too quickly.

Another whistle signal – and the match was in progress!

What a fight it was!

The teams carried the ball or kicked it with their feet, depending on what was most favorable at that moment. The scene changed constantly, with no pause or rest between grabbing, running and racing… attacks upon attacks. Soon I figured out that each team was trying to carry the ball over their opponent's goal line through the opposing strikers. They did this by running, shooting, throwing and passing the ball, fast as lightning. I also began to see who the better players were, but on the whole, all twenty-two men were such splendid players that it would be difficult for me to highlight any one in particular.

And so, I took in my first American football match as a spectator. Due to the extremely fast pace, I often mixed up the names of the players, despite the big numbers on their backs which you could check in the program. The first half of the match was over before I could come to my senses.

It was a hard, but absolutely "fair" fight… and, for me, incredible to take in. What self-discipline and athletic training must these players have in order to play this hard and continue to show good sportsmanship!

It was clear at the half-time break that the spectators expected the second half of the match with double the tension. One team would have to win… and, victory came for the Fordham players… our team! The Rams defeated the Mustangs!

Here is how it happened: When the first Fordham player carried the ball over the goal line the first time, there was a deafening applause by whistling, trumpeting and loud cries. I have never heard anything like that before! I felt as if I was in a haze.

Fordham now led by three points. That is not much, but at least more than the team from the south had, as their forwards had not carried the ball over the goal line even once. Seeming to make up for it, they now started an attack which almost took the audience's breath away. What a fire those athletes from the south had in their bones! They were driving the ball here and there extremely fast wherever they found the tiniest gap in the Fordham line. However, the Fordham players fought with all the might they had against the furious attack of the Mustangs.

I noticed that Fordham carried their name – the "Rams" – rightly. Suddenly, the Fordham center forward broke through with the ball on his foot! All at once the countless spectators went wild, jumping from their seats. Hats went flying through the air, trumpets and horns sounded, and the center forward was running and running, still with the ball. He drove it forward faster by carrying it. About fifteen meters from the goal, there were suddenly one, two players from the south approaching him. He dropped the ball to the ground where he kicked it with a hard but wonderfully precise shot over the crossbar between the two uprights.

What happened next can hardly be described… the whole stadium almost fell into ecstasy! That play had gained four more points, which meant victory!

What nerves must that player have had! His overjoyed comrades almost crushed him to death for his performance. There were only a few more minutes to play. Fordham University won, seven to zero.

Our Roman guests were very satisfied with that afternoon excursion. The same was true for me!

That extraordinary match of athletes had a great impact on all of us. We marveled at the amazing suppleness and power demonstrated by those sportsmen. My interest for those young people spurred me to want talk to any one of them. So, the next day, I went to one of our university athletes whom I knew well. He was a young man with the figure of a Hercules, and at the same time had just as well-developed manners and education. I asked him for a short interview. He received me very kindly and agreed to inform me about everything I should like to know.

First, I asked: "What is the relationship like between the athletes and other students here at the university, and in the American colleges?"

He answered: "Our position among the other students is good, by all means. We are friends with the other students and don't feel separated from them in our daily life." He added: "One might think that we athletes are less respected than the others because we engage in physical exercises, whereas the others concentrate more on spiritual questions. But that is not the case. On the contrary, our comrades seem to be even proud of us, especially when we emerge victorious in matches against other universities or colleges."

I replied: "Once one of the professors told me the same. And he expressed it in the following way: 'The other students,' he said, 'are really proud of their athletes and look upon them as a kind of heroes of their institution'."

"Yes, it is really like that," confirmed the young student.

"Now I want to ask you another question," I continued. "What do you do to maintain your mental and physical fitness, in order to achieve such athletic performance?" I was very much looking forward to his answer, I must say, for I was still amazed by what I had witnessed the previous day in the stadium. I admired not only their endurance and agility, but more so, the mastery of the body and the great spiritual discipline which I saw there. All of that made a great impression on me, the old gymnastics teacher.

The young athlete replied: "Dear Sir, we do nothing particularly special. We make a point of being in the fresh air as much as possible, and we get plentiful exercise. Furthermore, we try to lead a life as simple as possible, avoiding any kind of unhealthy consumption. Needless to say, we utilize gymnastics and train in practice matches as much as possible. Most importantly, we work to get the body under control, teaching it to obey, so that none of us hits the wall when it really matters."

"I can understand all that very well," I replied. "Is there a special diet you follow?"

"We subsist on the same food as anyone else. There are, however, two foods which we prefer to all others – if I may disclose them: namely, milk and spinach. That is the whole secret, Dear Sir!"

"Noteworthy," I thought to myself. "The simplest is always the greatest!"

NONNI IN AMERICA

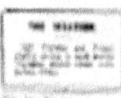

CHAPTER 39

GOODBYE TO NEW YORK

At different times during my stay at Fordham University, I was visited by American newspaper reporters who were curious about my world trip and my impressions of America and the American people. A few days after the interview, the article could be found in newspapers around the city. I admired the proficiency and skill of these American reporters.

On one occasion, the receptionist of the university came to my room and said: "Two journalists have asked for you. They are waiting in one of the parlors."

"Very well. I shall go and see them," I replied, and I went to meet them.

When I entered, both gentlemen greeted me politely and asked if I would permit them a few questions about my impressions of New York and American life. I agreed, of course. We sat down at a round table in the middle of the room. We talked briefly at first about the weather and similar subjects, but after a few minutes one of the two got up and went towards the window, saying: "Please excuse me, Sir, while my friend conducts his interview."

That seemed to me quite natural, and I had no reason to object. I reasoned that the gentlemen probably belonged to two different newspapers and therefore wanted to speak with me separately, to avoid publishing the same story in both papers. Thus, I did not pay much attention to the reporter sitting by the window. Glancing toward him now and then, I noticed he busied himself with a small box. I did not consider it any further.

The interview went on for a while. The gentleman at the table asked many questions about my journey and my stay in New York. I tried to give him satisfactory answers, and apparently was quite successful. The gentleman by the window waited patiently without interfering. All the time, he fiddled with his box. I felt a bit sorry for him, imagining how bored he must be; but then, it would soon be his turn, after all.

After the first gentleman finished, he thanked me kindly for a completely satisfying interview. Now I expected his friend to question me equally thoroughly. But, to my amazement, he rose, put his box under his arm and shook hands with me, saying: "I, too, am quite satisfied!" Furthermore, he thanked me for the interesting information I had given his friend, and indicated he was leaving.

"Excuse me," I said, "But I thought that you, too, might want to ask me some questions."

"No, Sir," he answered. "My friend and I are business partners. You have provided us with ample material, and we thank you very much."

At that time, I did not know what he meant. However, I was to find out – to my great surprise! The next day, a famous New York newspaper was sent to me. I found the article about me, immediately. There was everything I had told the one gentleman at the table the day before – precise, and well-written. Then, I discovered that was not all... for, in the middle of the text were photographs of me! Each showed a completely different facial expression... joy, pain, anxiety, amazement, doubt… and, to me, the most peculiar gestures. Below each photograph was printed exactly the phrase which had accompanied my corresponding gesture or expression.

This was a completely unknown concept to me. I was astonished beyond measure to see how American reporters work!

One such caption was: *"For God's sake! What are you thinking?"* So I must have said during the interview, and apparently made the corresponding face. Another image showed me laughing, under which read: *"I had the time of my life!"* In short, the paper printed everything I said with the corresponding face to match the story. The result was a row of photographs with rather funny facial expressions, paired with words which I had uttered unsuspectingly.

It now became clear to me that the gentleman by the window was taking my photograph as I sat with the other gentleman at the table. Any time I spoke excitedly or showed a rise in mood, he took my photo, and his partner would provide the corresponding words later to be printed under the picture.

This was either a good chance to become famous quickly, or a way to quickly lose support in a strange country – depending on what is said and what the journalists make of it! I must say, regardless of all else, that the American interviewers treated me well.

Following that interview, the time to wrap up my stay in New York drew near. I would soon prepare to leave my friends at Fordham University and in the big city. The generous and extremely amiable Rector Gannon, and all the professors at Fordham University, had treated me with the greatest affection, and all made my stay in New York as pleasant as possible.

I surveyed in my mind how my journey would proceed from this point on. From New York, I would travel to California by train across the American continent. Making a straight line, the journey from New York to San Francisco would last five days and five nights. But I did not want to go there directly. I intended to make more of a curve, so that I could see parts of Canada along the way. I would therefore head northwest from New York to Chicago, then take a direct train from there to the Canadian province of Manitoba. There, I would visit two flourishing cities: Winnipeg, in the English-speaking section, and Saint-Boniface in the French-speaking part. I had agreed to lecture in both cities, but there was another, more significant reason that Winnipeg attracted me: my dear, younger brother Fridrik lived there with his children and grandchildren. In fact, Winnipeg was home to several thousand other Icelanders as well. Of course I would want to visit my own brother, and my fellow countrymen!

Over the years, I had received many letters from men and women who had been my playmates in Iceland, over seventy years ago, who now lived in Winnipeg. Like me, they left Iceland many years ago, only they had migrated from Europe to Canada. What joy to be able to meet up with those dear childhood friends and former playmates after such a long time!

From Winnipeg I would travel to San Francisco, passing through Denver, the flourishing capital of Colorado. The city is a bit younger than me, for when I was born in the year 1857, Denver did not yet exist; but now, it has more than two hundred and fifty thousand inhabitants. This came to my attention one day when I was still in New York, and received a letter which read:

"Dear Nonni! I have heard of your trip around the world. Please make a stop-over in Denver en route to California, and be my guest for a few days. Sincerely, Your old friend and schoolmate, A.W. Forstall"

I accepted his invitation with great pleasure. Forstall and I had been schoolmates and good friends when I attended secondary education in Amiens, in the North of France, from 1871-1878. Mr. Forstall has since become a great scholar and has lived in Denver for many years.

Thus, I envisioned my itinerary going forward. Right now, it was time to ask the rector how much I owed for my three-month stay.

"What's this?" the generous man began. "Are you really leaving us already?"

"Unfortunately, yes," I answered. "I have much planned ahead. I would be quite glad, Rector Gannon, to stay longer, but I am afraid it is impossible. I have so enjoyed your hospitality these three months. You have given me the opportunity to get to know many American youth and the American way of life!"

"In kind, we thank you!" replied the rector. "You have given so many lectures on the country and people of Iceland… and, first and foremost, you have given our youth here insight into the European world and European youth. We owe you many thanks. There shall be no talk of any money owed on your part!"

Thus, this rather important matter was settled for me before I could ask, in an extremely noble and generous way! I could only thank him from the bottom of my heart, repeatedly.

And so, I left New York in the middle of December to continue my journey to sunny

NONNI IN AMERICA

California via Canada – greatly treasuring in mind and heart all the splendid and beautiful things which I had enjoyed with my dear American friends during my three months at Fordham University in New York.

CHAPTER 40

NEW YORK TO CHICAGO

It was time to leave my friends in New York City; the car which was to take me to the train station was already at the door. Rector Gannon had asked a reliable man to drive me to the station and help me to my train once there.

Hardly had I settled into the car when a young man came running up. I had seen him recently before, at some point, so he was familiar to me. He asked: "May I accompany you?"

"With pleasure!" I replied, and helped him get in alongside me. We began to chat as we drove off. He asked: "Are you going on some excursion?"

"Yes, but this time it will be rather long."

"Longer? You aren't leaving us, are you?"

"Yes, unfortunately, you have guessed rightly," I said. "I must leave New York to continue on my world trip."

"You mean, you won't be coming back?"

"I am afraid that's right. I am on my way to Japan, after all. But, should I ever return to New York, I shall definitely find a place in Fordham. I could not think of a better or more pleasant accommodation."

The young man looked at me with big eyes and said: "I had no idea that you were leaving now." After a short pause, he added: "What is your next stop?"

"Chicago," I answered. "There, I shall have a stopover of several hours. Then, I will continue on to Canada via St. Paul…"

"—To Canada? In the middle of winter? Do you know that Canada is very cold?"

"I have heard that," I responded, "but I don't worry about the cold, because I am healthy and very hardy."

He continued, "I have heard that you are past eighty – is that really true?"

"Yes," I answered, smiling. "But, let me put your mind at ease. I feel as strong today as I did sixty years ago, when I was twenty. I come from a family whose men and women lived to very old age."

I was touched by his kindheartedness and interest in my well-being. I did what I could to reassure him, but he still seemed concerned about my welfare.

After a short pause, he asked me: "Where will you go in Canada?"

"I shall go to the province of Manitoba."

"Which city will you visit there?"

"I will stay a few days in Winnipeg, where I have been asked to give a few English lectures. Afterwards, I shall visit the French city of Saint-Boniface, where I shall give a few lectures in French."

Now, the kindly young man gave me information: "Winnipeg is a very young city of about two hundred and fifty thousand people, and Manitoba is fertile with cornfields. Where else will you be going?"

I was pleased to continue as requested. "From Winnipeg, I shall go to Denver, Colorado, where I will visit a friend from my childhood for a few days. I have not seen him for almost sixty years! From there, I shall go to San Francisco, California, where I shall stay a bit longer."

"I can understand why you want to stay longer in California – that is a true paradise, with many beautiful things to be seen! Have you also got friends in San Francisco?"

"Yes," I said. "As I stayed here in New York, I shall stay at the university in San Francisco. The rector there, Harold Ring, is an excellent and amiable man. He has invited me very kindly to stay at his university as long as I wish."

"Wonderful!" remarked the kind young student. He continued: "Does he know you already? Perhaps he is also an old friend?"

"No, we have only just become acquainted," I replied, "and that is just the beauty of it. I only wrote him a letter telling him that I was making a journey around the world, and that I would like to stay in San Francisco for a few weeks. I asked him if I could stay in his university during that time. That was all. He said I may stay as long as I wish."

"You must be happy to accept this invitation," remarked the young man, "because there are so many beautiful things to be seen in California."

"Yes!" I replied. "But, I don't want to abuse his hospitability, especially since he offers it so freely. I suppose that my stay at the university of San Francisco will be as long as my stay at Fordham University in New York."

"Nobody here in America would regard that as an abuse of hospitality," the young man assured me. He glanced through the window and said: "In a few minutes we shall reach the station!"

Once there, our driver had us wait for him at the entrance to the station while he took care of everything that was necessary. He checked in my luggage and bought my tickets. Then, he showed me to my train, even to the car in which I would travel the whole journey to Chicago. He spoke to one of the porters on duty and commended me to him. And then, the driver returned to his car, leaving me there. As there was still some time before the train's departure, the friendly young student and I chatted more on the platform.

I said: "I am glad to have your company, even up to my very departure! I am so grateful at how polite and friendly the Fordham students have been towards me the whole time of my visit."

The young man looked surprised as he said: "Do you think that I am one of the Fordham students?"

"Certainly, yes," I said. "Don't you study at Fordham University?"

"No, I don't. I have never studied at that university!"

"Oh, my!" I cried. "I was certain that you were one of the Fordham students! Where have we met, then?"

Smiling, he said: "My parents invited you for lunch about two months ago. Later, I accompanied you back to the university."

Suddenly, as if scales fell from my eyes, I recalled that amiable family. There were so many different and new impressions which flooded me daily during my time in New York! So, that kind young man was someone else! Hastily, we renewed our former, actual acquaintance, and continued chatting until we heard the piercing whistle signaling the imminent departure of the train. I pressed my young friend's hand firmly and boarded the splendid Pullman car, where I stood by the window waving goodbye to my friend for as long as we could see each other. Then, I found a comfortable seat.

The huge train rolled calmly and sedately at first, and later, faster, into the swath of evening, which was getting darker and darker. Porters in white uniforms moved efficiently back and forth along the brightly lit car. They were widely known for their excellent service on American trains.

I felt at ease, even though everything was so new and unusual to me. I knew that I could settle in for a long ride in this splendid American train car. I would leave the train only after arriving in Chicago, for just a few hours, and then I would continue on another big express train up to the border between the United States of America and Canada.

But here, for the time being, I sat in that palatial train, surrendering to my moods, feelings and reveries.

The train rushed through the dark night. Most of the seats in the car were occupied. After a while, some of the porters entered our car and transformed the entire place into an extraordinarily fine and comfortable bed chamber!

How did they do it? It seemed that, in no time, these men somehow created a whole row of nice beds and placed them, rank and file, on both sides of the enormously long car. I observed closely, and soon discovered that all these beds had been hidden very skillfully in the walls of the Pullman car – so skillfully that, during the day, one could not have noticed them. They all were already made up and furnished splendidly.

Even after converting our car for sleeping, our space was still quite the noble salon. The only difference now was each side had a new row of niches in which we would sleep. I was amazed by the skillfulness of the American people.

A young French passenger, who was seated near me, smiled and said: "*Ces lits nous invitent et nous tendent les bras...* (Those beds are inviting us with open arms)!"

I replied: "*Vous avez raison, Monsieur, et bientôt nous accepterons cette invitation* (You are right, Sir, and soon we shall accept that invitation!)"

Those few words began a very pleasant conversation between the two of us. When the young man noticed that I spoke French, he moved next to me, and we chatted for a while in French about our journey, according to French manners. Both of us were travelling to Canada; he, to the French part of that vast country, which is almost as big as all European countries together.

"I am coming directly from Paris," he said, "and I am travelling to Montréal to conduct some business there."

"You are making a great detour!" I observed.

"I am doing it on purpose, in order to see something more of the world."

"Aha!" I said, "I am doing the same!"

After he had told me a bit about his business, he wondered: "May I ask where you are from, and where you are going?"

"I am also coming from Europe, from Paris like you," I told him. "But my business is totally different from yours, and my journey, too."

"You make me curious," he said with a friendly smile. "Are you going beyond Canada?"

"Oh yes," I replied, "much further."

He looked at me questioningly, followed by a short pause. Then he said: "Where will your journey go beyond America?"

I was glad to enlighten him: "I am visiting Canada only for a very short time, as I have relatives and friends there. Afterwards, I will go to California for a few weeks, to see more of this country and her people. I intend after that to travel to Japan and stay there for about one year. My return trip to Europe will be via China and India."

"The length of your journey is astonishing!" said the young Frenchman. "You must have substantial business to conduct!"

"Yes, certainly," I replied, "but that business is solely to see each country, as for years I have wondered and heard such marvelous things about them. I hope to tell my countrymen about the journey when I return, and even write a book on my experience. Does that sound desirable?"

"I think so," confirmed the young Frenchman. "Then, you must be a writer," he said.

"Yes… on the side," I answered.

"And, you are making a journey around the world like one of my fellow citizens!"

"Do you mean the famous Jules Verne?" I interrupted.

Amazed, he exclaimed: "Yes! Do you know Jules Verne, too?"

"Why should I not know him?" I answered. "I have not only read his books, but I have also lived in the same city as he did. There, I met him personally, visited him and talked to him. I have even spoken with him about the journey which I am undertaking now."

"Talked to Jules Verne, about the journey you are undertaking? That is almost hard to believe…" he mused.

"I don't hold that against you," I said, smiling. "It is true, nevertheless."

"Jules Verne died more than thirty years ago… but you have talked with him about your present journey?"

I explained: "I spoke with Jules Verne more than sixty years ago, indeed about my present journey, because even then I had already begun planning this journey in my head."

"Where did you talk with him?" he asked, still amazed.

"In Amiens, in Picardy, where he lived at that time."

"Yes, that's where he lived," said my companion, "… and there, a beautiful monument was erected in his honor."

"I have seen that monument, too," I responded. "It is located on one of the splendid boulevards of the city."

My new friend insisted I tell him how I came as a young boy from Iceland, via Denmark, to Amiens, and how I met Jules Verne there and talked with him about my journey around the world. What amazed the young Frenchman most was the fact that it took so long before I was able to realize my dream of traveling around the world. I endeavored to explain to him in short how everything had fallen into place in the end.

Then, as we were both growing tired, we called it a day, said goodnight to each other, and prepared for bed.

NONNI IN AMERICA

NONNI IN AMERICA

CHAPTER 41

AN ADVENTURE EN ROUTE

The young Frenchman and I went to our berths. However, I could not devote myself to sleep just yet, even though the many impressions of the day rendered me quite tired. I could already hear the rhythmic tones from several berths suggesting that many of my co-passengers had slipped into refreshment of sleep! Still, I wished to look out into the dark, mysterious night for a while. I found a quiet, solitary place at one of the car windows, where I sat and gazed out.

What did I see? Only opaque, sinister night shadows... yet, it was deeply moving to behold. I stared into that incomprehensible darkness for quite some time.

After a long while, I startled involuntarily at the emergence of a sharp, golden beam, which vanished as quickly as it had appeared. We had probably passed a brightly illuminated structure. Afterwards, only opaque darkness again, which was extremely creepy. I remained in my seat without moving and surrendered to my moods and sentiments, until finally I went to my berth. I switched off the light, said a short evening prayer, and a few minutes later was sound asleep in my splendid Pullman bed. All the while, the train carried us north at a terrible speed.

The mood gave rise to spooky dreams, which made for me their own amazing adventure.

As I slept, it began to feel like someone had seized my arm, and was shaking it. I could not see anybody, for it was very dark in my small berth.

"Who is there?" I shouted, rather dizzily.

The answer was: "*Ne craignez rien! C'est moi, votre compagnon de voyage* (You don't have to fear anything! It's me, your travel companion.)"

"But why do you awaken me? Is there anything going on?"

"Yes, something quite extraordinary. If you want to see it you have to get up quickly and come with me in the aisle, between berths. Then, you will see something you have never seen before."

I jumped out of bed and quickly wrapped myself up in my long dressing gown. My French friend guided me toward the window where I sat before going to bed.

"Look out!" said the young Frenchman.

I discovered to my great horror a huge flame, exactly where we were heading, still at a great distance. Looking closer, I discovered still more similar flames around our train. These luminous flames were moving, and approaching us quickly.

My travel companion said: "Those are brightly shining, immense snakes!"

I could see more clearly these snakes were approaching us from everywhere out of the sinister shadows, hissing and fizzling. I opened the window and looked out. It appeared that our train was one, long, giant snake, burning brightly at great speed.

"What can this be?" I asked the young Frenchman.

He answered: "I don't know… I only know it's there."

The smaller, shining snakes had almost reached us, and it seemed there would be a terrible crash. "We must be lost!" I shouted.

"Yes, that's what I am thinking too… *Nous sommes perdus, perdus, perdus* (We are lost, lost, lost…!)"

I was paralyzed with fear, but when I recovered my voice, I repeated: "We are lost, *perdus, perdus, perdus*…!" – just as the young Frenchman had done.

And then? The inevitable collision failed to happen. Instead, robust hands embraced me. I opened my eyes to see the kind face of our sleeping car attendant, who assured me we were not in danger, but that I had only been dreaming. .

The friendly Pullman car porter beheld me with great concern and compassion, asking: "Are you ill?"

I replied: "No, I will be fine."

He asked if I needed anything, and I said no, thanking him for his compassion.

With a friendly nod he left the berth.

I made myself comfortable in my bed again trying to think about what had happened. It became clear to me that the cause of that dream had been the fatigue and excitement of the previous day. I managed to fall asleep again, and, by morning, every trace of the peculiar dream vanished.

As I awakened and readied myself for the day, the porter came through to announce breakfast being served in the dining car. He added that we would soon arrive in Chicago, and therefore, it was recommended to have our breakfast immediately. So, we began filing to the dining-car as our train sped onward.

I heard another passenger say to his neighbor: "This countryside is so much different from the one we passed yesterday, isn't it?"

I looked through the window and saw that, indeed, everything was completely different.

Now, for miles around, one saw many dwellings: farms, houses of all kinds… even small towns and villages. Yesterday, our surroundings had more resembled a big desert.

"You can tell that we are nearing a big city," remarked one of the passengers.

Soon the dining car filled up, and there was much cheer among our many companions. Everyone seemed glad we would finally have a long stop-over in Chicago.

At breakfast, the young Frenchman joined me again, greeting me: "I hope that you had a good night!"

"I had a rather unusual night," I answered, and I described the dream in which he played such an important role, even unknowingly.

The young Frenchman and I sat alone at one of the smaller tables, and continued our conversation after breakfast.

"Are you going sight-seeing in Chicago?" he asked me.

"Oh, no," I said. "I won't have enough time, unfortunately."

"Will your stay be that short?" he continued.

"My next train departs in a short time after we arrive," I replied. "I will be traveling on to St. Paul and Winnipeg."

"I cannot linger either," said my new friend, "We shall have to say good-bye to each other here on the train, before our arrival in Chicago."

First, however, we enjoyed breakfast, and then prepared ourselves for the stop-over in Chicago.

At last, our train stopped in the giant station, in the middle of the megacity of Chicago. My French friend and I got out and said good-bye to each other on the platform. He had to hurry downtown, whereas a porter brought me to a very spacious and splendid waiting room where I would wait a few hours for my second train.

CHAPTER 42

STOP OVER IN CHICAGO

When I entered the waiting hall, my eyes beheld rich furnishings in the typical American style. A row of giant, smooth marble columns bore the heavy ceiling. Those columns were so solid that it would take at least two men to wrap their outstretched arms around just one of them. They made one row, from wall to wall, through the entire waiting room.

High up, on one end of the room, was a balcony that served as a gallery of sorts. Every ten to fifteen minutes, a man appeared, and it seemed that he sang out a solemn melody to the people in the waiting room below. I did not understand the words, but I surmised his song proclaimed the arrivals and departures. The solemnity of his voice was so striking that the people around me commented, for instance: "That announcer might be trying to imitate the Pope in Rome standing high up on his balcony to bless the crowds on St. Peter's Square!"

I stayed there about two hours until the arrival of the train to St. Paul and Winnipeg was proclaimed. I quickly headed toward platform with the big express train bound for Canada, first hiring a porter to take my luggage. On our way there, I asked him: "Is it far from here to Winnipeg?"

He told me, "From here to Winnipeg by express train, you need at least a whole day and a whole night."

"Then, it is as long as from New York to here," I remarked.

"Oh, yes, it is that far."

I said, "Please, choose a good car for me then!"

"The cars here are all good," he said with a smile, "but I shall look for a comfortable seat for you in the train."

He did keep his promise when I boarded the train. The porter chose an excellent seat, which would serve me well on such a long journey ahead. I was eager to travel to the far north, after all, up to the immensely vast British Dominion of Canada. I wished to be as comfortable in the elegant car as I could!

I need not describe the luxurious furnishings in this train. It is sufficient to say it was in no way inferior to the New Yorker! It felt as if I was in a beautiful salon with big windows on each side. I had a brilliant view in all directions, and on a nearby table lay many daily newspapers and magazines in many languages.

It did not take long for the train to start moving. We first passed through the magnificent city of Chicago. There were many interesting sights: big, monumental buildings, wonderful gardens and parks, and vivid American street life. We soon left the city and passed the famous Lake Michigan, at whose banks the city of Chicago is situated. Then followed rich and vast landscapes as the splendid train rushed faster and faster towards St. Paul. On our way we would pass through several American states, or at the very least, touch their borders: Iowa, Wisconsin and Minnesota, to name them.

Such beautiful scenery was unknown to me. While I gazed out at these natural wonders flying by, the restaurant manager appeared to invite the passengers to lunch. Everybody started the long walk through the many cars up to the last car, the dining car. As I was on one of the first cars, the walk was rather far. I admired the order, cleanliness, and exemplary facilities in each of these American railroad cars we passed through.

At long last, our row of hungry passengers reached the dining-car. It was especially spacious and furnished in the most comfortable way. Waiters served each of the many small tables, and everything happened in exemplary order.

Each table sat four persons. By strange coincidence, my table mates were a Frenchman, a German and an American. Despite our different nationalities, we got along very well. The American excelled in calmness and noble rationality, such that one might have thought he was of British descent. The German and the Frenchman tried to outbid each other in telling jokes. The gentlemen even teased each other a little now and then, in the most discreet and friendliest way – but always with perfect tact. As one example, I will cite the following little episode: The Frenchman asked the porter to bring half a bottle of white wine. The servant rushed off and soon returned with the ordered bottle. "Where does that wine come from?" asked the Frenchman. To our surprise, the porter answered: "From the Swiss colonies!" And he showed the bottle to the Frenchman. The label bore the words: "From the Swiss colonies."

"From the Swiss colonies!" repeated the Frenchman, amazed.

Then he translated the words in the French language: "Des colonies de la Suisse! Where are these colonies of Switzerland?" he asked, astonished.

The porter, of course, did not know.

All four of us looked at each other questioningly.

"Are there Swiss colonies at all?" asked the Frenchman. "And, above all, colonies delivering wine?"

For a few moments, we sat there at a loss.

Suddenly the German untied the knot and said: "Whatever may be the truth about the 'Swiss colonies', one thing is for certain: the Americans are clever enough to get hold of wine even from colonies which do not exist!" – and, smilingly, he shot a glance at the American.

We all laughed, and the American laughed most of all. My German-French-American table company was extremely lively and interesting!

When lunch was over, the dining car emptied, and the passengers returned to their seats. We sped onward toward our destination, which we should reach the following day.

TAUCHNITZ EDITION

COLLECTION OF BRITISH AND AMERICAN AUTHORS

VOL. 2743

LETTERS FROM HIGH LATITUDES

BY THE

EARL OF DUFFERIN

IN ONE VOLUME

LEIPZIG: BERNHARD TAUCHNITZ
PARIS: LIBRAIRIE HENRI GAULON, 39, RUE MADAME

The Copyright of this Collection is purchased for Continental Circulation only, and the volumes may therefore not be introduced into Great Britain or her Colonies. (See also pp. 3–8 of Large Catalogue.)

CHAPTER 43

A CANADIAN ACQUAINTANCE

On returning to my seat, I looked at a map of the region through which we were travelling. I identified the stretch we had remaining until St. Paul, and then the way from St. Paul to Winnipeg. It was much longer than I had thought. The only unpleasant aspect was not having a companion with whom I could talk in a brotherly, amicable way. The young man from Paris parted ways with me in Chicago, as you know, and in his place were new, unknown passengers on this train. It looked like I would remain by myself on this long leg of the journey.

While this thought was going through my head, something uncanny happened, which I least expected. A lone young man, about sixteen or seventeen years old, whose seat was only five to six steps away from me, stood up at this moment and came to my seat. He greeted me politely and said: "Sir, will you permit me talk with you for a few moments?"

"With the greatest pleasure!" I replied.

My new companion sat down immediately and began a lovely conversation between us. More uncannily – something I had not expected – he, too, spoke in French, did not know any English.

First, he introduced himself explicitly: not only verbally, but handing me also his business card. His name was Pierre.

"Excuse me if I disturb you, but in the dining car I heard that you are going to Canada – that is, to Winnipeg, in Manitoba. I live near Winnipeg, in the St. Boniface neighborhood. Although I belong to the French-speaking area, I do know some of the English-speaking inhabitants of Winnipeg, including your brother Fridrik whom you mentioned during your conversation with your table companions. I am most eager to make your acquaintance!"

"In that case, you are doubly welcome!" I said. "I am completely unfamiliar with both Winnipeg and St. Boniface. Perhaps you could be so kind as to share some useful information for me to have during my stay there?"

"That would be my pleasure!" replied the good boy.

I immediately liked this young man.

Listening to Pierre was delightful, and he likewise seemed to enjoy my stories. He asked encouraging questions, such as: "If I am not mistaken, you said earlier that you don't know much about your brother Fridrik's life in Winnipeg. He came from Iceland, situated in the North Atlantic Sea, didn't he?"

"Yes, that's true," I replied.

"Then both of you are Icelanders?"

"Yes!"

"In that case, you already know that many Icelanders live in Manitoba, in the city of Winnipeg."

"I surely do, but only generally," I answered. "There are a few thousand Icelanders in the city of Winnipeg, as I understand, and a good number elsewhere in the province of Manitoba. There are some additionally in the United States."

"How is it," interjected the boy, "that so many Icelanders came to Canada, especially the province of Manitoba?"

"I will gladly explain that to you," I replied. "Do you know – at least by name – of the great English politician Lord Dufferin?"

"Yes, Canadians know who he is. He was governor general of Canada for a long time. He was also vice king of India for many years. In the end, he was British envoy in Paris."

"I see you are well informed!" I said. "But you may not know that Lord Dufferin came to Iceland in the year 1856, when he was still a young man, on his own ship. That was one year before I was born. He spent some time there, traveling through the whole country, diligently studying the history and the literature of the Icelandic people. He was so moved by it that he wrote a nice book upon his return home, entitled 'Letters from High Latitudes'.

"He had fond feelings for Icelanders throughout his life. When he became governor general of Canada, he invited the Icelanders to come there, promising them his help and protection. In those years, many Icelanders wanted to leave for various reasons. Many accepted the invitation, and in the years from 1870 to 1880, thousands of Icelanders emigrated to a new homeland in Canada.

"Most of them went to the fertile province of Manitoba, where few had settled from outside the land. There, they founded – together with English and other emigrants – the city of Winnipeg, which now has about two hundred and fifty thousand inhabitants. Among the first Icelandic immigrants there was my youngest brother Fridrik, who now lives with his family in Winnipeg."

My new French-speaking travel companion thanked me sincerely for this short explanation about my countrymen in Canada, but his thirst for knowledge had not yet been completely satisfied.

He asked: "Why did you not emigrate to Canada with your brother?"

I answered: "Fate led me in a different direction, and I have not regretted it. I left Iceland the same year in which Fridrik emigrated to the New World, but I emigrated to France, and have spent a great part of my life there."

"Your brother Fridrik must be a total stranger to you!" my friend mused.

"In a certain way, yes, because we have been separated for about seventy years. He has spent his life in North America, whereas I have lived in various countries of Europe. We do stay in contact via mail now and then."

"So, you have not seen each other for seventy years?"

I answered, "We have seen each other only twice in our entire lives."

The boy seemed stunned by that thought. He looked at me questioningly. After a short pause, he whispered: "What a tough lot!"

I could see that he wanted to know a bit more. Therefore, I continued: "The first time I saw my brother Fridrik was when he was still a baby, napping in his cradle. I did not see him again until he came to Iceland about six years ago."

"Six years ago? And in Iceland?" Pierre was amazed. "Please, tell me how that happened!"

"It's my pleasure! It was actually a bit strange. In 1930, I returned home to Iceland to take part in the festivities on the occasion of the millennium of 'Althing,' the Icelandic parliament. At that time, I spent a few weeks in Reykjavík, the capital of Iceland.

"One day, when walking through the city, I met a small group of travelers who had come from Canada to celebrate the event. Suddenly, one of the gentlemen looked at me closely. He was an elderly man whom I did not know at all. He greeted me and asked in English: 'Excuse me, Sir, are you not the author Jón Svensson?' – He had recognized me from a photo.

"I replied: 'Yes, Sir, I am.' Then the stranger said, this time in Icelandic: '*Jeg er Fridrik, broðir þinn,*' (I am Fridrik, your brother.) You can imagine my amazement and emotion! We thereupon stayed together for a few days."

"A strange fate!" repeated young Pierre several times.

I continued: "Now, I shall see my dear brother Fridrik for the third time, this time in Winnipeg. Most probably, it will be the last time."

We sat together for a long time, chatting about life in Manitoba and especially in Winnipeg. It was his turn to give me information.

"About a generation ago," said Pierre, "the land upon which Winnipeg is situated now was vast and undeveloped, but unusually fertile. The indigenous people moved about the land with their tents. Nowadays, this land has been developed into a real granary, a fertile, cultivated land."

He then switched back to the subject of my brother. "You will stay at your brother's in Winnipeg, I suppose?"

"No," I said, "his house would be too crowded. For that reason, he has booked me a special flat in a first-class English college, at least for my nighttime lodging. During the day, I plan to spend most of my time with Fridrik."

"I know that college," said Pierre. "It is an excellent school near your brother's house."

And so, we both sat, having a good time as the train rushed north, faster and faster, towards the province of Manitoba. Towards evening, we reached the important city of St. Paul. We stopped there only a short while before continuing on to Winnipeg. For that last stretch, we needed the whole night.

NONNI IN AMERICA

CHAPTER 44

ARRIVAL IN WINNIPEG

With the train racing northward at incredible speed the whole night, we reached the English-Canadian city of Winnipeg by morning. After we eased into the main station and stopped, I got off quickly and – if I may put it this way – fell directly into the arms of my dear brother Fridrik, who had been waiting for me at the platform. He seemed exactly the same as the person whom I had met by chance six years before on the streets of Reykjavík.

My brother led me out of the railway station to a car that was waiting for us. There I had the pleasure to meet one of his daughters, a very charming young lady, and one of the professors of the Canadian college as well. I got into the car and was taken by the Canadian professor to my accommodation. We hardly arrived at the college when two gentlemen from the press greeted me – and whose curiosity I had to satisfy, of course. There were two photographers with them, snapping my picture. Who knows how they had learnt so quickly of my arrival in Winnipeg, or that I would be staying at this Canadian college?

I cannot tell you how well I was looked after at this college. They did all they could to make my stay as comfortable as possible. I had the opportunity to give short lectures now and then to the students living there. More importantly, my dear brother Fridrik and I were inseparable during the eight days I stayed in Winnipeg. He introduced me to my fellow Icelanders as often as possible. Through his connections I was invited to several festive gatherings, meetings and lectures. As the Icelandic-Canadians still used our mother tongue, I found myself speaking in classical Old Norse-Icelandic. I had not spoken Icelandic for sixty-six years, mainly because I have always been among foreigners. It was a great pleasure to hear it now and enjoy its beautiful tone. The sound entered deep into my soul, awakening all my dear childhood memories.

It seemed like each of my experiences there flowed into the next.

NONNI IN AMERICA

I spent my first night in the Canadian college quite peacefully. After breakfast the following morning, I sat in my room, writing a few notes in my diary. Suddenly, I heard the bell in the floor under my room. Shortly afterwards, I heard footsteps leading to my door.

"Perhaps it is a visitor for me?" I thought. I had gradually become accustomed to being visited as soon as I had arrived at a new place.

The knock on my door suggested I was correct. I called: "Come in!"

The door opened, and there stood my brother, Fridrik. I rushed to greet him, then I offered him the chair next to my desk. He sat down and we started to chat: "What's up today?" I asked him.

"Plenty!" he said, smiling. "At noon, you will pay a visit to the Archbishop of Winnipeg, Msgr. Sinnott. He has invited you for lunch, and you simply must accept!"

"For sure!" I replied. "It is a great honor for me. But how will I find the way?"

"I will see to that," said Fridrik. "Around 11:30, a car will come to take you to the bishop's residence, and you will arrive shortly before 12 o'clock. You will stay until around 2:30, when I have arranged another car to pick you up and take you to see a friend and fellow countryman Rev. Björn Jonsson. He, too, has invited you for a short visit. Finally, I will order a car to pick you up and bring you to our home. Then, you will be able to rest a little, for you will surely be tired after all this!"

That was the plan for December 10th. However, my brother was not finished. "For tomorrow, Friday 11th December, your agenda has also been set."

"Can you describe what I will do?" I asked my brother.

"Certainly: At 12 o'clock, you will be my guest, together with our fellow Icelander, Rev. Dr. Rögnvaldur Pétursson. He is the president of the Icelandic National Association here in Canada. A good number of Icelandic gentlemen and ladies will also be with us, including Mrs. Eleonora J. Jónsdóttir..."

When I heard that name I startled in amazement. A mental picture from my earliest youth emerged in my memory. I interrupted him and asked: "Did you say Eleonora J. Jónsdóttir?"

"Yes, certainly," replied my brother.

"Approximately how old is she?"

"She might be between seventy and eighty years," replied Fridrik.

"And, where in Iceland did she grow up?"

"In Akureyri, on the Eyjafjörður."

"Good Lord!" I cried, as my hunch became clear. "She is one of my former little playmates from Akureyri! In the years around 1869 and 1870, so, about sixty-five or sixty-six years ago, I remember a dear little girl who often played with us. Most of us were between seven and ten years old at the time. Her father was a respected man in Akureyri."

Fridrik smiled. "Everything you say fits perfectly. It must be Little Eleonora of the old days who is here now, only now a bit older, just like the two of us."

You can imagine how moved I was by this idea, and how eagerly I looked forward to the coming luncheon at my Fridrik's home.

Memories of my youth in Akureyri on the Eyjafjörður came rushing back, and in spite of my eighty years, I felt more like the little Nonni of nine or ten years. After lingering another moment, I turned again towards my brother and asked: "Are there any other plans for today and tomorrow?"

"I have not told you all of them yet," he replied. "There is still something rather important."

"What might that be?" I asked, curiously.

"It is an invitation for tomorrow night. A very wealthy Icelandic lady, Sigurbjörg Currie, has invited you to a festive dinner at 7 p.m., together with some gentlemen of her acquaintanceship. This will probably last until midnight, as is the custom. Now you know what to expect, more or less, these first two days," said Fridrik, concluding the program designed for me. But, alas, that was not the only duty waiting for me; my brother had barely said goodbye to me when there was again a knock on my door.

"Come in!" I cried – a bit more loudly than usual.

The door opened, and one of the college professors stepped in.

"Good morning!" he said as he approached. "May I talk with you for a moment?"

"Of course, it would be my pleasure," I said. "You are welcome."

The gentleman sat down and pulled a letter out of his pocket.

"That letter was delivered to me just now," he said. "It comes from St. Boniface."

"St. Boniface … That is the neighbor town, isn't it?" I asked.

"Yes, you are right. And, as you know, it lies in French Canada. We are in the English section. The border between French and English Canada runs in close proximity."

"Yes, I have heard about that. Is the letter written to me?"

"No, Sir, but it concerns you."

Then he took the letter out of the envelope and read it to me.

"*Please ask the Icelandic traveler staying at your college to visit us the day after tomorrow and give a lecture in our high school — of course, in French.*"

The professor looked at me questioningly while he put the letter back into the envelope.

I hastened to assure him: "I will accept their invitation with great pleasure. But please, consult with my brother about the time of my visit, since he has many other plans with me already. I will also need a car to take me from here to St. Boniface."

"All of this will, of course, be done with much pleasure," assured the friendly gentleman. "So, the French lecture is agreed?"

"Yes, that will be fine with me," I replied.

"Many thanks for your kindness!" said the professor. Then he got up, pressed my hand and left the room.

I looked at my watch and saw that I still had plenty of time till my brother came to take me to the Archbishop, so I began preparing what I would say at my lecture in St. Boniface.

I had not quite finished this when there was again a knock at my door. Whatever could I do? "Come in!" I shouted, as usual.

The door opened, and this time my visitor asked if I might be willing to give a few lectures to the junior and senior students of Winnipeg, in English this time.

"I shall do this with great pleasure," I answered, "but I admit that my English is not perfect."

"Oh, you are mistaken," the gentleman chided. "Your English is impeccable." Yet I knew exactly what that praise meant: To the polite Canadians, every foreigner speaks an 'impeccable' English, even if it is anything but good.

Then my visitor got up, thanked me again and left the room. I was on my own again.

While I sat there, I heard bright laughter and loud shouts outside. What might that be? I got up, went quickly towards the window, and looked out.

Directly in front of me was a big playground covered by a thick sheet of ice, and many students were frolicking happily. Others rushed out of a nearby school building to join them. Several had already put on their ice-skates and were darting to and fro with tremendous speed. It seemed the young people were running wild on their skates while each was armed with a heavy stick. As fast as lightning, as if life itself was at stake, they chased after a small, black object, trying to hit it with their sticks.

I had never seen such a game before. What might it be?

I heard someone passing in the corridor outside my room. I opened the door and saw a friendly young man carrying a few books. I asked him: "Excuse me please: What are those young skaters doing on the playground over there?"

"They are our students, playing a match."

"Does this match have a name?"

"Yes, they are playing 'Hockey,' our national game."

"Is it always played on skates?"

"In winter, yes, as long as we have ice. Our playgrounds are covered with ice during the whole winter."

"How do you cover the entire playground?"

"When the weather gets below freezing every autumn and winter, water is sprayed onto the playground until a thick ice crust has formed. Then, hockey is played on that ice during the whole winter. Our students are excellent skaters and hockey players. Have a look how they are playing below!"

Indeed, there was cheerful life on the playground below. I had never seen more skillful skaters in my life.

"You are right," I said, "those young people are excellent players."

"Yes, that's true! Our Canadian hockey players are highly esteemed in Europe. For that reason, they are often invited to England to teach the youth there how to play hockey properly."

I thanked the friendly young man for his explanation, and as he left the room, I saw my brother Fridrik already waiting in front of the door.

"Are you ready?" he asked me.

"Yes, I have waited for you."

"Then we are all set," said Fridrik. "In ten minutes, we shall go to the Archbishop."

"Look here," I said to Fridrik, leading him to the window.

"Oh, yes," he said. "Those are the hockey players of the college. They are professionals."

"Is it true that they even teach hockey to the English youth?" I asked him.

"Sure," he replied. "Every year, the English teams fetch some of our best hockey players in order to learn from them."

When the time came to leave, I put on a thick winter overcoat and went down with Fridrik, to where the car was waiting. We got in and departed.

During our ride, Fridrik turned towards me and said: "I think that you will like the archbishop. He is very affable. Although most Icelanders are Protestants, and he is a Catholic, he loves us. You will notice it yourself soon enough."

"I am glad to hear that," I said. "Normally, I am not used to finding people interested in Iceland, nor us Icelanders… even less, people who appreciate us. In general, people look at us as if we were Eskimos."

"That might be the case in other areas, but not here in Canada," said Fridrik. "Here, we are respected. And this holds especially for Archbishop Sinnott."

"I am glad… and, I'm eager to learn about all the Icelanders living here. More than four thousand Icelanders are said to live in the city of Winnipeg, as I understand."

The car stopped after a short ride to the Archbishop's palace.

NONNI IN AMERICA

CHAPTER 45

EXPERIENCES IN WINNIPEG

A servant received me at the entrance of the Archbishop's mansion and led me upstairs to meet him.

The Archbishop received me with the greatest kindness. He asked me a few questions about my fatherland and my journey around the world. I asked questions of him, as well; I was especially interested in his opinion on the Icelanders in Winnipeg, and in Canada in general. He was full of praise for them. "They number, in every aspect, among the most capable immigrants," he said, and he repeated various times: "The Icelanders are splendid people!" I could not imagine a friendlier and more amicable gentleman than that dear church dignitary.

When my visit concluded, I went back to my brother, who took me then to meet Rev. Björn Jonsson, one of the most respected clergymen of the Icelandic community. I spent a few hours with Rev. Björn, learning from him many interesting details about the Icelandic settlements in Canada and the United States of America. Afterward, Rev. Björn helped me get back to my brother Fridrik's home. There, I had the pleasure of meeting Dr. Rögnvaldur Pétursson, a highly educated gentleman and president of the Icelandic National Association in Winnipeg.

I cannot say how happy I felt to be among my fellow citizens, and how pleased I was that they maintained solidarity in speaking in our mother tongue, which I had not heard since I was twelve, but preserved as my dearest treasure – namely, the memory of my mother. After so many years away, it felt as if I was in my beloved fatherland again, in Ultima Thule. I had that feeling especially when Rögnvaldur Pétursson brought me along to the meeting of the Icelandic National Association and dinner afterward, where the most important personalities of the Icelandic Canadians gathered.

Many attendees gave speeches during dinner. I was asked to give one too, in my Icelandic mother tongue. And then, I was able to reunite with my playmate from Akureyri, little Eleonora – who had become a venerable woman. When we recognized each other, we talked about distant old days, the times when we played together in the small town of Akureyri at the Eyjafjördur. She reminded me of my youthful pranks. How much had changed in us and around us!

The old Icelandic hospitality was strong in Canada, as seen during my next visit – to the house of my compatriot, Mrs. Sigurbjörg Currie. At 7pm I accompanied several Icelandic gentlemen to the home of this Icelandic widow, who made our nearly five-hour visit extremely pleasant and interesting. During dinner, I noticed that one of the guests was always served special dishes. I discovered Mrs. Currie heard that one of the gentlemen preferred vegetarian dishes, and as she did not think his giving up meat was a mere hobby, she made sure to serve that guest meatless dishes, while all the other guests had theirs with meat. I was amazed at that tender consideration on the part of my compatriot.

Eventually, the day arrived to visit St. Boniface in French Canada.

Sure enough, it began with a knock on my door. Supposing that it had something to do with St. Boniface, I called in French: "*Entrez*! (Come in!)"

The door opened and an unknown gentleman came in.

He made a deep bow and said: "*Bonjour, Monsieur, pardonnez-moi, si je vous dérange?* (Good day, Sir, I hope I am not bothering you?)"

I pointed to a chair and asked the gentleman to have a seat.

When he sat down, he said: "I am one of the teachers in the French college in St. Boniface, and I've come to take you there. You were so kind to promise us a visit and a lecture."

I answered. "It is my pleasure to keep that promise."

"We ought to depart from here immediately," the professor said. "The rector of this college will go there with us."

I took my hat and winter overcoat, and left with the unknown gentleman. The rector of the college, and my brother Fridrik, were already waiting downstairs beside the car. As soon as we were all in, we drove off.

Being unfamiliar with the region, I imagined our drive would be quite a journey. After we had driven about a half hour, I asked the French-speaking gentleman: "How long will our journey from here to the French-Canadian college take?"

"We are nearly there," he said with a smile, "We have just reached St. Boniface." I remembered my young Canadian travel companion had told me that the two cities of Winnipeg and St. Boniface were close to each other. I saw, to my astonishment, that we were already at the French-speaking Collège St. Boniface.

Being an Icelander here did not make me a rare guest, with so many of my fellow citizens living in neighboring Winnipeg. Therefore, I surmised my lecture should not concentrate on Iceland, but more about my impressions of Paris and London, or perhaps Germany, Holland, and England, as well as my voyage across the Atlantic and my stay in New York. Furthermore, I might talk about my plan to journey across America to California, and about everything that would follow.

"Here in Canada, it is bitterly cold in the middle of December," said one of the gentlemen, "but when you get to California around Christmas, you will experience springtime temperatures. California is a paradise. You must stay there more than just a few days."

"That is my intention," I said.

The rector opened the door and talked with someone for a few minutes, then he turned towards us and said: "*Tout est prêt pour la conférence*" (Everything is ready for the lecture.)"

So, we got up and followed the rector to the big Banquet Hall of the college, which was packed with listeners. In the middle sat the students; at the very back, and on both sides, sat the professors and various residents of the college. It was a lively and expectant assembly.

Now, I had the floor. When everything was still, I began my lecture. They gave me a good hour. I spoke of some experiences of my long and varied life, and about events which happened to me on my trips through so many countries. I have never avoided challenges, but always marched toward each destination in the straightest line possible. I am grateful to the Lord for my desire to explore and for the walking courage which He has infused into my blood. I have been blessed to tell my stories to old and young folk alike, bringing pleasure to many people – as uncountable letters have confirmed, and as I have experienced during the hundreds of lectures I have given. I was accustomed in Europe and in the old-cultured countries to having people enjoy my storytelling, but it is one of the greatest surprises of my life that people of the New World also enjoy my stories. That surprise has grown as I have gotten to know the New World with its huge buildings, its machines, its splendor, and its dimensions. Even these modern people, and their modern world, understand me.

When my lecture concluded, the audience thanked me with applause, according to custom. I promised that I would give another lecture in that college if ever I returned to the province of Manitoba. I stayed and chatted for a while until it was time to return to Winnipeg.

That visit in the beautiful college of St. Boniface would not be my only one: I was invited to give a second lecture shortly thereafter, followed by an invitation for dinner by the Most Reverend Bishop. I marveled at the kindness and attention of those dear people, who as yet barely knew me. An extremely friendly young Irishman, Mr. Murphy, who was engaged to an Icelandic girl, gave me a lift in his car when I needed to go from Winnipeg to St. Boniface. On each occasion, he showed me sights of both cities. He did not let me leave Manitoba before I paid a visit to his house as well.

I cannot describe how happy I felt to be at brother Fridrik's, and with his family. Always and everywhere, they took care of me with the most touching kindness and love.

NONNI IN AMERICA

NONNI IN AMERICA

CHAPTER 46

ENTRUSTING MY NEEDS

As my days in Winnipeg came to an end, I had to think again to continuing my journey around the world, with this incredibly long stretch across the giant North American continent still being only the first leg. After all, an American train traveling nonstop, day and night, at top speed, would need five days and five nights to reach California on the Pacific coast in a straight line from New York on the Atlantic coast: a journey of five days and five nights simply across ONE country!

I thought it would be a good idea to review my remaining itinerary for the details and specifics I would need to know. I went to one of my compatriots who had lived in Winnipeg for many years and knew a lot about the area. As I heard he hoped to have me as a guest in his house, I visited him, and was received with the greatest cordiality. He led me into his study so that we could talk, undisturbed. After we sat down, he began by asking me: "Have you got your ticket with you?"

"Yes, certainly," I replied. "Do you want to see it?"

"Yes, please, if you'll allow me."

I took the ticket out of my pocket and handed it over to him.

After checking it thoroughly, he asked: "You bought this ticket in New York, for your journey to San Francisco, in California?"

"Yes, certainly," I answered.

"I am a bit puzzled by the route this ticket has you taking." He paused, and then he explained: "First, you went from New York to Chicago; then, from Chicago to St. Paul, and from there, to Winnipeg. From Winnipeg, you will go back to St. Paul, which is correct; but then, this ticket takes you back to Chicago, and from there to Denver, and finally to San Francisco. It is incomprehensible that you would return to Chicago, as that is a detour of two entire days, for an unnecessary amount of money."

"That _is_ incomprehensible!" I said.

"We cannot do anything about it, for the time being," he said. "The ticket was printed erroneously in New York, and you have already paid your fare. You may have no choice but to take that strangely long route. You will definitely reach San Francisco, only much later than it should have been."

I was surprised that such a mistake could be made by the otherwise very practical Americans. I put my ticket back into my pocket again. My compatriot suggested I address the matter at the railroad station. He felt they would certainly reimburse the fare I had spent unnecessarily. I promised to do so, curious to see how that matter would turn out. Then, I changed the subject and asked my compatriot for a few details about living conditions in Winnipeg and in the province of Manitoba.

He answered: "We Icelanders, as well as the others who have settled here, are very satisfied with our surroundings. Winnipeg has experienced a wonderful development. The same holds for the entire province of Manitoba."

"Is life in Winnipeg easy, and affordable?" I asked.

"In fact, it is. But consider how our living situation has developed here," began the gentleman. "Fifty or sixty years ago, Winnipeg was a tiny little village with two to three hundred inhabitants. The entire province of Manitoba was like an incredibly vast desert where only a few bands of natives roamed about in tents. The Europeans felt unsafe, not knowing if the natives were hostile or friendly. Today, there are more than three hundred fifty thousand inhabitants in Winnipeg and its suburbs, and that expansion is still going on. The city abounds in big and splendid buildings, and the economy flourishes here better than nearly anywhere in the world. The countryside has turned out to be one of the most fertile and largest wheat-lands of the whole world! The little village of Winnipeg with its former population of two to three hundred has now the biggest and richest grain market of the whole British Empire. Yes, one can say without exaggeration that Winnipeg is a wonder city of great progress. Winnipeg has become the biggest commercial and industrial city of the entire Canadian west, as all experts agree."

I couldn't help being amazed when I heard all that.

"But," I asked, "are those facts and statements accepted in serious circles?"

"Yes, Sir," replied my compatriot. He got up and fetched a big book about the North American economy, opened it and read to me the corresponding information. There was no doubt. Everything I had heard there was true indeed.

After we had chatted a bit more about the remarkable development of this city, I bade him farewell and returned to the college. I would stay only one more day and two nights in Winnipeg, and then continue my journey to California and the Pacific Ocean.

My departure was on December 16th. However, the situation with the train ticket troubled me. It was more and more clear how illogical this route was. They must have made a great mistake when printing the ticket at New York train station, and as a result, I would have to spend extra days crossing the United States unnecessarily. Therefore, I went to the Winnipeg railroad station to inquire about the matter. When I got there, I asked one of the officials to lead me to the station master, who received me very politely.

"Sir," I said, showing my ticket, "I am on a journey from New York to California, and purchased this ticket in New York. May I ask if everything is okay with it?"

The station master took the ticket and looked at it carefully.

Confused, he asked, "You have come here via Chicago and St. Paul, haven't you? And now, you want to continue your journey to California – via Denver, Colorado. Is that correct?"

"Yes, Sir. I will depart for St. Paul on December 16th."

"Your ticket says that, from St. Paul, you will go back to Chicago. Have you any reason to return to Chicago?"

"No, Sir, none at all."

"Well, in that case, it is absolutely wrong, because you would travel a full day in the wrong direction, namely, back towards New York. From St. Paul, you should be routed to Omaha – not Chicago."

I asked: "Why on earth was I issued this ticket, for which I have also paid more than needed?"

He answered: "The gentlemen in New York must have had a bad day. But you need not be angry. When you get to St. Paul, I will make sure you will hear from the gentlemen in New York, and we will correct this situation."

I could not quite understand his words. "Sir, what do I do now?"

The gentleman answered in a very friendly way: "Go from here as planned, to St. Paul, on December 16th. There, the railroad station personnel will speak with you about the correct route. Don't worry, I will ensure that everything will be okay again. Your journey will continue, and your overpayment will be refunded faithfully." His words calmed me completely, although I was not quite sure how he had the authority to promise me this.

Encouraged, I began making the last preparations for my long railway journey. I would depart on the huge train from Winnipeg to St. Paul on December 16th in the afternoon. I said my goodbyes to friends and acquaintances, and had my luggage settled and ready to go. Yet, even on the day of my departure, I had a last invitation for lunch by the gracious bishop of St. Boniface – so, I went there first. The bishop and his priests were extremely friendly, and I felt very happy in their company. Then, it was time to leave and to go to the station. I was accompanied by my brother Fridrik, Professor Kelly from Winnipeg college, and two professors from St. Boniface college.

At 6.30 pm I boarded the train and left the distinctive city where I had felt so happy in the last few days. The beautiful Canadian train started southward, first slowly and cautiously, then faster and faster, bound to cross again into the United States of America.

That train felt like a rolling magic palace. I took my customary exploratory walk through the vast and extraordinary cars. The high and broad aisles were trimmed with polished mahogany, shimmering brownish, dark red. In such splendor we sped forward the whole night, expecting to arrive in St. Paul around eight o'clock the following morning. I looked for our beds, but one could not discover where they were hidden. Only a bit later a robust porter appeared and pressed a row of buttons, one after the other, which were installed on both walls of the broad aisle. Immediately, a great number of nicely made beds sprang out of the walls, and the wide aisles were transformed at once into grand bedrooms!

At the same time, the dining car was being prepared for us. The loud bell soon signaled our invitation to dinner.

The dining car filled up quickly, and in a cheerful atmosphere, the passengers enjoyed a late meal. This time, I stayed on my own, better to observe everything that was going on around me. After dinner, most travelers remained for a while in conversation with each other before getting ready for bed. I would have felt more at ease if my ticket situation could be resolved. It said, after all, that I should take the next train the following morning to Chicago. However, the station master had said not to board that train, but to entrust my needs to station personnel in St. Paul. How could they know to approach me and direct me instead to the train which would take me to Omaha? Would the American railway authorities be able to put me on the right train? Would they really be waiting for me, without my having to draw their attention? Or would I miss the next leg of the journey as a result of the mix-up?

I would have to submit blindly to that mysterious support of the American railway directorate. You no doubt understand how the matter troubled me. Would it not be more reasonable draw their attention to my ticket as soon as possible, to avoid being stranded? The railway directorate in Winnipeg had explicitly advised me otherwise, and I hoped I understood them correctly.

NONNI IN AMERICA

NONNI IN AMERICA

CHAPTER 47

IN THE HANDS OF THE AGENTS

My anxiety accompanied me as I entered my berth to lie down and rest. The train continued its rush through the pitch-black night with tremendous speed. Despite the trembling and rattling of the huge railway car, we tired and sleepy travelers found our wide beds exquisitely cozy. I felt sleep take hold and slid gently into dreamland. Indeed, once more, I was seized by force of the ghosts of my dreams, in various and extremely dramatic adventures, the entire night.

Many fellow passengers were already up by the time I awakened. I got up, dressed, and carried my luggage to the aisle so that I could leave faster when we stopped. As I looked out I saw our train was entering a rather big city! I turned towards a traveler standing beside me and asked him: "Do you know the name of this city into which we are pulling right now?"

"Yes, Sir," he said, "it is St. Paul. Many people will change trains here. Perhaps you, too?"

"Yes," I answered, "I shall have to change here."

Shortly we passed another long train standing motionless on the tracks. I asked the same gentleman: "Do you know which train is that?"

"That is the train to Omaha, and it is about to leave."

"That is my train…!" I cried, completely terrified, "I have to go to Omaha!"

"You must not lose a second," said the gentleman, emphatically, "You must jump with your suitcases from our train as fast as possible!"

I didn't need to be told twice! I quickly dragged my two suitcases to the little stairs leading below. A traveler opened the door and helped me out, as I did not have the time to find a porter. However, as I was still getting out, the train to Omaha whistled and began pulling off!

In mortal terror, I ran with my two suitcases after the ever-faster moving train as it departed, desperate with almost superhuman strength. Of course, I could not reach it. I cried with all my might: "Stop! Stop! - - - I need to go to Omaha…! I need to take that train! I need to take that train!"

However, all efforts were in vain. The locomotive trundled happily forward, and the conductor did not hear my calls. The train to Omaha slid forward, faster and faster.

Completely desperate, I placed my two suitcases on the ground and called to a porter standing nearby. "Please, help!" I repeated. But apparently the porter did not hear me.

In that moment, however, a hand placed firmly on my shoulder startled me. I opened my eyes and saw the porter… that is, the porter of my splendid Winnipeg train, looking at me kindly as I lay in my berth among the other travelers, all of whom were also resting in their comfortable beds. My fellow passengers turned toward me in concern for my loud cries which awakened them from their sleep, and I came to realize this was one more of my dream-adventures. Since the beginning of my world trip, this was my third time being haunted by such peculiarly lifelike dreams. Unfortunately, I had disturbed the sleep of many of my fellow travelers, but all of them gladly forgave me. Our kind and efficient porter helped calm everyone's confusion, starting with mine. Soon we were all asleep again, and the second part of the night was as calm as the first had been restless.

The following morning, we got up at the appointed time, and soon were called for breakfast. Afterward, between eight and nine o'clock, we finally reached that important junction, St. Paul, where – according to my ticket – I was to go to Chicago, though in reality I knew it should be Omaha.

At 8:15am, our train pulled in the station of St. Paul and came to a halt under its huge, vaulted ceiling. One of the porters came and helped me get off the train with my two heavy suitcases.

I asked him where the train to Omaha was.

"It has not yet arrived," answered the obliging porter. "It will pull in after approximately two hours," he added, "so you will have a stop-over here."

Now I would know if the gentleman in Winnipeg had been right as far as my onward journey to Omaha was concerned. I only had the ticket to Chicago, and he had told me the American railroad company would take care of the error. I did not even have to draw its attention to my faulty ticket; a representative of the railroad would approach me and show me the right way.

Due to my European ideas and experience, that seemed to me impossible. But I was willing to test it. So, I walked back and forth among the many passengers moving about, and left the worry solely to the American railway men.

I did turn once to one of the people surrounding me and asked him: "Excuse me, Sir, I want to go to San Francisco in California. Can I get there via Chicago?"

"You can do that, without any doubt," was his answer. "However, it would be a great detour."

"So I have heard. But now another question: I am a foreigner from Europe, and I fear that I got a somewhat faulty ticket in New York. I am completely unfamiliar with how to proceed. How can I solve that problem?"

"In such cases," replied the gentleman, "the railroad personnel will help you with greatest ease. You have nothing to fear and you don't need to worry about anything. There is a special facility called the 'Passenger Department' with officers called 'Passenger Agents.' If travelers are having problems, they provide immediate support. So, you have nothing to fear, even if your ticket should not be quite right. The Passenger Agents will fix everything."

I had to admire the efficiency and reliability of these American facilities. I was determined to wait until those mysterious Passenger Agents approached me to help. It is my pleasure to inform my readers that I did not have to wait long. About an hour later, two official gentlemen in nice uniforms came towards me and greeted me politely.

One of them addressed me: "Good day, Sir! May I ask you to show me your ticket?"

Out of caution I asked: "Please allow me the question: Who are you, Sir?"

"We both are Passenger Agents. We help passengers when they have any problems."

I got my ticket out of my pocket and showed it to the friendly agent, who checked it and asked me: "Have you got a special wish to travel via Chicago?"

"No, I haven't."

"In that case, I would suggest that you go via Omaha."

"I would prefer that, too."

He went with me to the station counter and ordered a new ticket from St. Paul to Omaha, then Denver, then San Francisco. I had to pay for that new ticket, even though I had paid the full price for the faulty first ticket in New York. I looked at the Passenger Agent questioningly. He understood immediately, and said: "You may send your first ticket with your mailing address to the railroad directorate in New York, and the money you spent on that ticket will be reimbursed to you immediately, no matter where you might be."

After I had considered that, I replied: "I am a foreigner and a complete stranger in this country. I am afraid I cannot handle that correspondence correctly, nor do I know the correct address in New York. Could you please settle that matter for me?"

"Certainly, it will be my pleasure. Tell us to which address the reimbursed money should be sent."

I thanked the gentleman heartily and said: "As I intend to stay in San Francisco for several months, the money should be sent there. My address will be the following:

Jón Svensson
Ignatius University
Fulton Street 2130."

They put the old ticket into an envelope, wrote a few words to the railroad directorate in New York, and added my address in California (where, in fact, the full refund was later sent).

Thus, the whole ticket affair was settled, and the rest of my long journey across the United States was completely secured.

I thanked the agents for their competent help, whereupon they turned their attention and help to other passengers.

After purchasing the new ticket, all difficulties were over, and soon I boarded the new train which was to take me to Denver, Colorado via Omaha, Nebraska, in just over twenty-four hours.

NONNI IN AMERICA

CHAPTER 48

ELEGANTLY ESCAPING DEATH

The train which was to take me from St. Paul via Omaha to Denver would be considered a first-class luxury train by any European.

Before boarding, I took an attentive walk along the outside. It was already impressive when seen from that angle! Strolling down the long line of imposing railway cars, taking a slow and leisurely survey, my eyes fell on an inscription written in big golden letters. It was printed in English, and the meaning was the following:

"Since the foundation of this railway company, not a single accident has happened with our trains."

Not once! Those words had a very soothing effect on me, as I had heard and read more than once that railway accidents occur more often in the United States than in most European countries, given the comparatively high speed of the American trains. That was certainly alarming, but this golden inscription reassured me.

Shortly afterwards it was time to board, and I did so with a particular joy and sense of security. The train's interior facilities were just as splendid and convenient as those in previous trains. Again, I felt as if I were in a magical palace. I was happy to find a seat next to a window so that I could enjoy my view the entire time.

Yes, I was happy and without any worry at all. I did not think of the proverb: "Don't count your chickens before they are hatched."

When all were comfortably settled, our impressive train took off with enormous speed in a southeasterly direction: first, heading to the beautiful states of Minnesota and Iowa, and then reaching the important states of Nebraska and Colorado.

My fellow passengers were very pleasant. In my proximity sat a young, distinguished- looking Japanese man with whom I conversed in English very pleasantly. I had occasion to notice for the first time how the Japanese honor old age. Being just over 80 years old, I found this young man paid me special attention. He told me that he had traveled through many European countries and observed each carefully. He best liked England, France, Germany, and Italy, even as he found the character of each nation different from the other. He named several pleasant attributes of each nation, offering no complaint toward any of them. Surprisingly, he did not speak much of Japan!

In the evening, the majority of our fellow passengers went to bed early. But my Japanese friend and I decided to take a long walk through the whole train. We admired the sumptuous furnishings in the different cars. The dining car was by far the biggest and most beautiful of all. It was furnished extremely tastefully and was so large that all passengers could be seated there comfortably at the same time. At the far end was a room where all food and dining provisions of the train were stored. A library and a magazine room were also installed there. All these beautiful facilities amazed us. We had never seen anything like it in the wide world!

After admiring the train's extraordinary facilities, we said "good night" to each other and went to our berths to get ready for bed. Soon a peaceful nocturnal silence surrounded the entire train. Had I known in advance what lay in store for all of us, I would not have gone to bed for anything in the world! Better I should have stayed up to be ready, in case of emergency. But none of us had the slightest idea of what that night would bring. I was drowsy and tired, and only wished for a sound sleep and a good rest. The strong shaking and trembling, whirring and roaring as the train wildly stormed along did not hinder my rest in the least; in fact, I fell asleep immediately.

I do not remember exactly how long that sleep lasted; but how I suddenly awoke in the middle of the night, I remember very well! I was lying in my splendid bed unsuspectingly, sleeping soundly and calmly… until a terrible blow hit me and my bed! In a flash, I opened my eyes, looking quickly to all sides, but only seeing pitch black. I was trembling all over in fear. The blow felt as if a strong person grabbed me with both hands and threw me roughly to the foot of my bed. The bedding had also been flung by the terrible impact. But that was not the end: the entire car kept shaking with exceedingly violent jolts and powerful blows. Loud shouts and cries came from my fellow passengers, which told me that they felt it, too.

"What is going on?" shouted a voice somewhere inside the sinister darkness.

"Perhaps we are being attacked!" cried another voice. Very loud gasps were heard from various sides as people considered this possibility.

"Does anyone have a rifle?" shouted someone over the din. Several men jumped out of their beds. The commotion grew louder and louder, and the possibilities felt very threatening.

I probably owed it to my somewhat advanced age, and perhaps also to my trust in God, that I did not get involved in that horrible excitement. I remained on my bed, not so much by deliberation, but rather the result of a certain instinct it seemed to me – in that impenetrable darkness – more reasonable to wait and see what the next moments would bring. Thus, I did not make any unnecessary movements, remaining still and yet ready to move if needed, – whereas those around me were moving like mad, to and fro. Then, everything became quiet as we noticed that the train had come to a halt.

"The train is stopped! What can that mean?" cried somebody near me.

"Something quite sinister must have happened," shouted still another, from one of the higher berths.

An eerie silence penetrated the whole car. The train started moving slowly, but then we felt the shock of being thrown forward, then backward. From outside, there were suddenly loud shouts and cries. Many tried to look out of the windows, but we could not see anything. The shouting outside increased sharply. I held on to the bed and tried to understand what was happening.

"Have we been attacked?" asked again another strong voice from somewhere in the car.

"It seems like it..." replied some other voices from around the windows.

However, nobody really knew.

Someone standing near one of the windows suddenly announced: "Something is going on behind the last car! People are moving back and forth in the shadows… but I cannot see what they are doing."

Now everybody leaned out of the window looking in that direction.

"It must be a fight!" several voices shouted in confusion.

"Impossible!" shouted another. "There are no attackers!"

There was an awkward pause. For a few seconds one did not hear any sound. Then, the first strong voice called out: "Behind the last car is complete confusion."

"Are they working?" someone asked.

"It looks like they are fighting a battle!" shouted another.

The guessing went back and forth between the various eyewitnesses in the darkness for about two hours. Things finally calmed a bit after that. Although the night was pitch black, there was a bright light from behind the last car of the train, and nobody could guess what was actually happening back there.

Finally, a group of people could be seen approaching our train from behind and boarding the rearmost car. The passengers in our car tried to get out and see what was happening, however, the doors were firmly locked. Suddenly, loud orders and commands could be heard, and then the train started moving again… first, slowly, and then faster and faster. Finally, we were moving forward with the usual speed.

As little as we knew, we passengers decided this signaled a happy ending to our ordeal. Some were amazed that we had escaped without injury. A senior gentleman shouted to me before he fell back asleep: "I'm glad you are still alive! I had hardly dared to hope! One thing is for sure: we have narrowly escaped death."

NONNI IN AMERICA

NONNI IN AMERICA

CHAPTER 49

AN APPETITE FOR DENVER

Almost all passengers had gotten up when the mysterious jolt took place. In the complete darkness, everything was in chaos; one did not quite know what to do, other than wait for information. When it was all finally settled, a loud shout came from outside: "There is no danger anymore! All travelers may return to their rest!" We breathed a sigh of relief and went back to our berths; however, in such complete darkness, it was nearly impossible to put oneself and one's things in order. Some people had difficulties finding their clothes and other small items, and others could not find their berths – or found them accidentally occupied by someone else. There were several mix-ups and misunderstandings.

Well into the night, many remained awake, exchanging remarks and opinions on the strange adventure. A few still assumed the train had been attacked, and the marauders had been beaten back. I listened with interest to their theories, but I did not express an opinion myself, being far too unfamiliar with American conditions. I contented myself that daylight would bring a full explanation. Meanwhile, we settled back into our beds as best we could, and soon most of us fell asleep.

After the disturbances and agitations of the night, many felt the need to sleep somewhat longer. Those who got up first waited patiently in our seats for the latecomers, hoping that we would soon be called for breakfast by the usual signal. But there came no such call, even though the time for breakfast had long passed by. Some of the gentlemen pulled their watches out of the pockets. When they noticed the time, they looked somewhat surprised.

One of the gentlemen stood up and said, "I shall go ask what is the matter." He went to the dining car, the big last car of the train.

After a short while he returned reporting the following: "There is no dining car any more… it broke down yesterday, and is lying beside the tracks, far behind us!"

The travelers looked at each other in silent amazement. After a pause, one of the gentlemen asked: "Where shall we have our meals today?"

The first gentleman replied: "I was told there will not be any meals. All food provisions had been in the dining car, and were lost in the catastrophe overnight."

"Aren't there any other provisions on the train?" asked one of the gentlemen.

"No. There aren't any."

There was another pause… and someone remarked: "We shall not reach Denver before tonight. Do we have to fast until then?"

"Yes," said the gentleman.

"But," said another gentleman, "can't one get any provisions on the way to Denver?"

"No," answered the first, "that is impossible, because there are no towns or villages between here and Denver. Our route is completely uninhabited."

Thus, we had to accept our fate, which we did with (more or less) courage and determination.

Soon we received detailed information about the nocturnal events. It had not the slightest thing to do with attackers at all. The unusually big and heavy dining car had collapsed, and the contents and provisions were lost.

I need not say that among the travelers there was a subdued mood during the rest of our day of involuntary fast and hunger. People spoke little, sitting there in silence, each in his own place. All seemed to be occupied by their thoughts. It brought to mind the story of the "Académie silencieuse" of antiquity, which I heard during my studies in France. Just as those academics sat silently around their table, so we too sat gravely and silently in our seats for the many long hours of this travel day.

As if the train felt pity for us, it rushed through the never-ending plains of Nebraska, reaching the flourishing city of Denver in the State of Colorado late in the evening. There, I was met by my childhood friend and classmate from old times, the French professor William Forstall, who had gone on to become a great and famous scholar – and whom I had not seen for more than half a century. He no longer bore the youthful countenance I held in memory, but now, in Denver, I found him a venerable old man who received me in the most gracious way. After greeting each other on the platform, we went into the station building.

The first thing I did was unfortunately very prosaic, but I will no doubt be forgiven: I ordered a double portion of porridge, together with a pot of milk, and ate hungrily. To my apology, I can say that I had almost fainted because of hunger and weakness. The meal restored me, and my dear friend took me in a car to St. Regis College, where he worked as a professor and had lived for many years. I was received with the warmest welcome and at once pressed to stay for a while. I was provided a nice apartment, where my every wish was fulfilled.

I was slated to give several speeches in the college and in the city. The college rector was goodness itself towards me. He drove me by car to various families in town, where I always was received kindly and spoke a lot. In the company of those dear people, I felt at home.

Professor Forstall was too modest to speak much about his life, but one of the gentlemen in the college told me, "Forstall is a widely known specialist in everything concerning chemical and physical sciences. From Denver, he consults miners and prospectors searching for gold in California and other places. They send him samples of their subterranean findings, stones, gold veins and other items. After close inspection, Forstall informs them if they should continue with their works and excavations. He is known all over the world for his scholarship." He was extremely loved by all who knew him, especially his students. Yet, he never spoke of his achievements. Once, he said: "Everything truly great must develop in the shadow, in poverty and simplicity – not by money or big advertisement."

I barely describe how happy I was to be in the company of my dear childhood friend, the now-famous William Forstall! But, as with the other stops on my journey, I would find myself preparing to depart once again, if I were to continue my trip around the world. Dear old Forstall and the rector brought me to the railway station on the last day, doing everything in their power to see that my travel would be good and comfortable going forward. I had in front of me the next leg, from Denver through the wonderful Rocky Mountains, to the second largest state in America, the paradise known as California.

CHAPTER 50

LAND OF SCENIC MARVELS

The next leg of the trip was one of the most interesting one could imagine, for it went from Denver through the rest of Colorado, and then through the states of Utah, Nevada and the paradisiacal California, up to the coast of the Pacific Ocean. Along this route is one of the greatest natural wonders worldwide, namely, the incomparable Rocky Mountains. Even my train ticket promised such a spectacle; there, in strange print, read the following:

> "Through the
> Rockies,
> Not
> Around
> Them"

I had only been a few days in Denver when I had to say goodbye to my new friends there. Shortly before my departure, the rector of the college said to me: "Your last stretch in America will probably be the longest, as it takes at least two days and two nights even on a fast express train. It will, however, be one of the most interesting routes, for you will travel directly through the world-famous Rocky Mountains. There you will pass through one of the longest tunnels in the world, and will cross the middle the famous Salt Lake, which is an extremely large body of water like the ocean, though located far inland."

You can surely understand how I was looking forward to that last portion of my trip across America with great expectations.

My dear friends in Denver accompanied me to the train station and saw that everything was in order. It was December 21st when I left, hoping to reach San Francisco just before Christmas Day. I boarded my train, which was just as exquisite as the other American trains.

This train was also extremely long – not because of an especially great number of cars, but because the cars of the train themselves were great in length. In fact, I do not remember having seen such long railroad cars ever in my life.

Soon, the signal for departure was given. With a last grateful farewell to my hosts, the beautiful train started moving, leaving behind the friendly city where I felt so happy. After a short while we hurtled forward with the tremendous speed which is usual for such trains, as by now I had come to know.

And so began the last leg of my trans-American journey.

In just over two days I shall see the beautiful paradise of California, I said to myself. *There, I shall be able to rest thoroughly from the many hardships of travel for at least two to three months.*

Before settling into my train seat, I made a brief visit to each of the long cars. There was probably space enough for several hundred passengers. I wandered slowly through this interesting train, looking at the facilities: each single car had space for twenty-four sleeping passengers ("Twelve lower and twelve upper beds," as a sign said in English). Additionally, there was extra sleeping space on upholstered benches.

When I returned from my walk through the train to my seat, I asked the young man sitting opposite me: "Excuse me, Sir, do you know how many cars this train has?" as I had forgotten to count.

"There are just over twelve cars," he answered.

"In that case, there is enough space for many hundreds of travelers," I mused.

"Yes, you are right," he said. "The train is almost full."

"Do you know if one has to pay an extra fee for a bed?"

"Yes, for each bed one has to pay eleven dollars extra."

I stayed mostly silent for a while after that, sitting in place and preparing myself for the last stretch of my long journey across the vast American continent. I wrote a short bit in my diary. Now and then, I exchanged a few words with the young traveler sitting opposite me, but I was much more introspective, filled as I was with the awe of realizing all that had transpired to bring me to this point.

After a while I noticed – at least it seemed to me – that our train was gradually beginning to climb upward. As I was not quite sure if my feeling was correct, I asked the young man: "Do my senses deceive me, or are we on an incline?"

"It is no deception," replied my counterpart. "We do climb these huge mountains. The Rockies are some of the mightiest mountains in the world."

"How is it possible," I continued to ask, "that the railways can ascend such tremendously high mountains?"

"It is made possible by building the railroad line in bold turns up these colossal mountains."

In surprise, I answered: "What a wonderful show of enterprise… Americans shrink back from nothing, and they are very audacious! Are there any tunnels on this route?"

"Yes," he answered, "there is one called The Moffat Tunnel. It is a little over seven miles long, the longest mountain tunnel in the United States of America. It was dug through the highest mountain passes over which the railroad line could not be built. But, all said, Americans would rather bridge the mountains rather than pierce through them."

I could very well understand that.

I liked listening to the friendly young American. But soon I wanted to go on another tour of the train. I said to my amiable neighbor: "I thank you very much for the valuable information you have given me. I am off to see more of this train, but I may have more questions for you. These American trains are of high interest to me because they are beautiful and practical at the same time. The more I observe, the more I find new and surprising details."

"Good luck with your expedition!" replied the young man, quite pleased. "I am available to help you with any further information."

So, I left the friendly young American for a while and headed back toward the last car, thinking from there I might have the best panoramic view of our surroundings. I was correct: there were windows not only on the sides, but also on the rear of the huge car. When I looked out, I saw a tremendously high and wide rock wall which we were passing in that moment. The color of that rock wall was peculiar: it was strangely piebald from top to bottom, black spots within the predominant field of white.

The wide view was white as snow, blotted here and there with pitch black, then other areas shimmering in all colors of the rainbow. It was a splendor without equal: silver, grey, crimson, cherry red, green, yellow, blue, orange, lustrous gold … I might continue endlessly, and even then I could not adequately describe how it looked in reality! I can barely find the words strong enough to express my feelings and my enthusiasm correctly.

On further exploration through the train, I found the railway cars of this train were even more beautiful and comfortable than I first thought. The next car was astonishingly bright. I saw it had large windows on all sides. I asked the first man nearby: "What sort of car is this?"

"Sir, this is the observation car," he answered. "From here you can have the best view of the landscapes through which we are passing."

I noticed pleasant music playing on a radio. Instead of continuing my walk, I sat down and listened awhile as I looked out at the wonderful view. It was quite tempting to stay there indefinitely, but the urge to explore was strong enough that I eventually continued my walk. I next entered the dining car, where the Restaurant Manager happened to be.

"Good day, Sir," he said. "May I invite you for a cup of coffee?"

I accepted this friendly invitation with pleasure. While I drank the coffee, we had a pleasant chat. When I stood to continue my walk, the Restaurant Manager said: "Sir, in about ten minutes we shall pass through the Moffat Tunnel. Perhaps you will want to stay here till we are through."

That seemed reasonable to me, so I sat back down. The manager was eager to tell me about that tunnel, and I was glad to stay and hear. I said: "The Moffat Tunnel must be quite significant, am I right?"

"I should say so!" he replied. "It is one of the greatest tunnels in the world."

"Do you know how long it is?" I asked.

"Yes, I do. It is a little over seven miles long."

"Then it is, as you say, one of the biggest worldwide."

"You will be pleased to see it yourself," the manager continued. "In Europe, you have a few bigger tunnels than our Moffat Tunnel. After all, the Mont Cenis Tunnel is over eight miles long; the Lötschberg and Gotthard tunnels are over nine miles long; and finally, the Simplon Tunnel is nearly twelve miles long. The Europeans love to build tunnels, while the Americans prefer to build bridges!"

I appreciated the man's sense of justice. Soon, the ten minutes elapsed, and our train entered the impenetrable darkness of the tunnel with a great roar.

When we emerged back into the light, the most beautiful and magnificent mountain landscape appeared before our eyes: mighty great rock walls, deep abysses, jagged rock and mountain peaks, in different shapes, reaching toward the sky.

One of the passengers exclaimed enthusiastically: "One could almost believe that a terrible fight took place here between Titans and mountain giants hurling rocks against each other!"

"Yes!" said another passenger. "Such a battlefield would have looked exactly like this landscape here!" Our train raced through this wildly torn and ransacked mountain world with terrible speed.

As one of the servicemen walked through our car, someone called out to him: "Will we remain on top of these mountains for a long time?"

The man answered: "We have just climbed the highest tops of the Rocky Mountains. Now, we begin descending, as you will soon notice."

So it was… yet, we continued through this mountain wilderness for a long time. There was little conversation as all eyes were directed towards the windows. Our fascination with the wonderful view was reflected in the amazed glances of the passengers. We went on like that for quite some time… on and on… and, none tired of watching!

Alas, as we descended this magnificent mountain world, the plainer became the landscape. The heights and hills grew gradually softer and the angular shapes gradually vanished. In their place came rounder hills, and instead of the terribly deep abysses, there were idyllic valleys.

At once we were startled out of our observations by the signal of a loud bell inviting us to the dining car! Without hesitation, we got up and started toward our dinner. Within a few minutes, all seats in the huge dining car were occupied. My table companion was a friendly-looking young man.
We introduced ourselves. "My name is Muramatsu," said the young man. "I am living in San Francisco, but I was born in Japan."

I was a bit astonished to hear a Japanese name, as his facial features did not especially appear Japanese.

I introduced myself too: "My name is Jón Svensson," I said. "I was born on the island of Iceland. I live in Holland, now, however."

We began to chat like old acquaintances. The friendly young man asked me questions about my journey, my person and profession. I, too, asked him similar questions about his life and circumstances. With the greatest frankness he answered all my questions. My joy meeting a Japanese man on the train was so great that I seized his hand and said: "I am on my way to Japan, your fatherland!" Mr. Muramatsu said in friendly reply: "I am pleased to meet a travel companion who wants to visit my fatherland. Have you been there before?"
"No," I answered, "it is my first journey to Japan. But I have heard a lot about Japan and the Japanese, and I have also read much about the

country and its population. I have learned to esteem and love your countrymen from afar… but now I intend to get to know the Japanese in person."

At first, he looked at me in silent amazement. Then he said: "I marvel at your interest in Japan!" He added: "Are you Icelandic-American?"

"Oh, no!" I laughed. "I am and will remain a true, native Icelander."

There was a short pause, and the young man said, "Wait a moment… Jón Svensson… Nonni?"

"How is it possible you know me?" I exclaimed in amazement.

He said, "I have come across your name in the American papers!"

I owed it to my American interviewers that the young Japanese from California knew me. You can imagine my joy in realizing this!

During the meal we continued chatting and got along excellently. I told him that I was on my way to California, where I intended to stay for several weeks, and from there I would travel directly to Japan.

"Is that the main reason for your journey?" asked the young man.

"Yes, it is. I wish to get to know Japan and the Japanese people so that later I can tell the Europeans about them, and thus can bring your culture nearer to the western youth and western peoples." I noticed that he would like to know what I had read about his fatherland, but he was too tactful to ask me directly. For that reason, I said: "I have mainly and especially read what the famous Francis Xavier has written about that wonderful country and that highly talented people."

"You have already learned a lot about Japan and the Japanese people. Now, you will be able to form your own opinion about the country and the people by your personal experiences and adventures. Being in California will aid you in learning about Japan as there are very many Japanese people there."

I was happy about this accidental acquaintance with that intelligent young man, for through him, I could begin learning all sorts of things about his fatherland and about his compatriots.

NONNI IN AMERICA

CHAPTER 51

ARRIVAL IN SAN FRANCISCO

Soon, we left the mighty mountains far behind us, rushing always with the same speed through rolling plains, where no trace of any kind of life could be seen.

That was especially the case in the most peculiar states of Utah and Nevada.

For hours we sped through "dead" land where neither animals nor people could be seen. There were neither any trees nor shrubs, neither grass nor flowers. Young Muramatsu said to me: "This is really an interesting piece of America, whose creation has not yet been finished."

When lunch was over, my Japanese friend was approached by a fellow traveler, and so we separated for a while.

By the afternoon, we finally came to a few stretches of land where little bits of life were stirring, starting with tufts of grass – but even that grass looked like coarse paper. I could not get tired of looking at this tremendously vast, strange, flat area, where not even the slightest change in the terrain could be discovered, neither a deepening nor an elevation.

"This must certainly have been where the ocean was in former times," I heard a traveler say to his neighbor.

"Yes, that's what I think, too," replied the neighbor. "I could imagine the bottom of the sea being like this."

This remarkable countryside made a deep impression on all of us. There was not much conversation. Most passengers silently mused in their seats, incessantly watching the strange landscape through which our train stormed with restless haste for hours.

A sudden, shrill cry of fear awakened us from our reverie, and everyone jumped up in fright. An elderly lady, on her own at the end of the car, shouted in despair: "We will drown! The train has gone underwater!"

Everybody looked out of the window...

... and, what did we see?

We could not believe our eyes. The land had indeed disappeared... and around the train was nothing but water! Could it be that the train had truly gone into the sea?

I, too, was stunned for a few moments. Most travelers in the car, however, seemed to know better, for several spoke to assure us: "There is no danger! We are on the causeway, crossing the Great Salt Lake!"

I calmed down on hearing that, because I remembered in Denver I had been told about this particular stretch of Utah. But those traveling this route for the first time, who had not been prepared for such surprises, might easily think in these first moments that our train had fallen into the sea.

All windows were occupied as everybody strained to see the famous Salt Lake. I hardly managed to find a seat near a window, but my Japanese friend Muramatsu was there with several gentlemen and helped find me a good seat. The view was exceedingly peculiar. Looking forward, we could only see a vast, shoreless surface of water.

"This is a huge lake after all," I said to my Japanese friend. "It almost looks like the ocean!"

"Yes, you can say that," he replied. "When speaking of making the trip to the Salt Lake, in California, people say 'Going to sea by rail'."

"That lake is just as salty as the ocean," I said. "How did they manage to lay heavy rail tracks across this vast surface of water?"

"They managed to do it because the Salt Lake is not very deep. Thus, it was possible to build a causeway right across the lake. That causeway was only made wide enough for a single train to run on it. If it had been made wide enough for two trains running parallel, the costs would have risen tremendously. However, at some points, double tracks have been installed so that, in case of emergency, the trains can pass each other."

Looking through the window, I saw that, indeed, the causeway only had space for one track. To provide stability, a seemingly infinite number of narrow wooden beams had been rammed deeply into the ground through the water – so it seemed to me. By that method, the whole construction acquired an unusual appearance. On both sides of the causeway, there were long rows of telegraph poles in the water. Their reflections made it seem as if they were hanging freely between heaven and earth.

In any case, our heavy train ran fast and safe through the wide lake toward the other shore. This leg of the journey was one of the most adventurous railway trips I had ever undertaken in my life!

After crossing the lake, our train hurtled forward many hours through a variety of landscapes: first, through beautiful mountainous areas; then, once again, through almost endless barren deserts. The nearer we came to paradisiacal California, however, the more life started to make itself known. At first, only a few tufts of grass could be seen. Then, small dwellings appeared, more like shacks here and there than residential neighborhoods. I also saw a horse, a very skinny and poor animal, moving about slowly and not having much luck finding food.

The further we moved on, the friendlier became the sky, and the temperature grew warmer – although we were still in winter! It was near the end of December, but one did not have to wear winter clothes. Behind the last car of our train there was a little platform. A young man sat there comfortably reading a book, wearing lightweight summer clothes!

The next day, the 23rd of December, we were to reach San Francisco.

As we got closer, the landscape turned more beautiful and the vegetation more luxuriant. Also, the dwellings we saw were bigger and bigger and more charming. Between them there were cute little villas and large-scale buildings. Finally, great miracles of wealth and human progress appeared: magnificent monumental mansions and huge palaces, flourishing gardens with rare trees and other plants, green velvet lawns and splendid flower gardens. We must have been close to the Pacific Ocean now! The air was mild with the scents of fragrant flowers and all the glories of the rich, blissful, sunny south. We had only to spend one more night in the train.

The next morning, between 7 and 8am, our train pulled slowly into the California city of Oakland, which lies across San Francisco. Only a narrow inlet separates both important cities. We disembarked our train and went to a mighty ferry, which in a few minutes devoured the big swarm of people and took us all across to San Francisco.

When I stepped off the ferry on the other side, a friendly gentleman approached me, greeted me politely and asked me to get into his car. I thought to myself that he was probably one of the professors at San Francisco University, where I was to live during my stay in California. I asked the gentleman if this was true.

"Yes, I am one of the professors," he said. "The university rector, Mr. Harold Ring, asked me to pick you up and drive you to San Francisco University." I got into the car and sat beside my driver. Then, I saw the streets of San Francisco for the first time.

We had hardly driven any distance when I saw in front of us a rather high hill. The street was in perfect condition, and on both sides stood big city houses, but the street was strangely steep. Yet, the car climbed the hill quickly, and at the same speed went down the hill on the other side. After a few minutes, we reached a second hill even steeper and higher than the first! The car climbed this hill as if nothing had happened, and then drove down on the other side at a very high speed.

Soon there was a third hill, high and steep, like the other two. Weren't we in the middle of a large city? I was amazed ... I had not imagined San Francisco like this.

I turned to my friendly driver and said: "Professor, I have never seen such a hilly big city in my life."

The professor smiled and answered: "You are not the first one who is astonished. There are still a great number of more such hills here in our city! Rome was built on seven hills, but San Francisco stands on several dozens. Our hills are an integral part of our city."

After a short pause I continued: "Aren't these hills an obstacle for the traffic?"

"Oh, no," replied the professor. Then he added: "I know that in Europe people think so, but our trams and our cars drive over these obstacles very easily as if they were not there!"

For me, this was something completely new. My first trip through this very beautiful city made the best impression on me. After crossing more hills, we finally reached Fulton Street 2130, the address of The University of San Francisco.

There, I was received by Harold Ring in the most amicable way. I was provided with two rooms, and the rector offered me to stay there as a guest as long as possible.

NONNI IN AMERICA

NONNI IN AMERICA

CHAPTER 52

RECEPTION AT USF

When I was well situated, I went to see the University Rector, Harold Ring. He received me very kindly, and during our conversation he asked me several questions about my journey.

"You wrote me from New York," he said. "If I have understood you correctly, you are making a trip around the whole world."

"Yes, Sir," I answered, "I am traveling around the globe, indeed, via America and Japan."

"And you started this journey in Europe?" he continued.

"Yes, Sir. I traveled on an English steamer from Southampton to the United States. Then, I crossed the American continent, from the Atlantic to the Pacific Ocean, finally reaching San Francisco this morning. From here, I shall travel to Japan on a Japanese ship."

"How long will you stay there?" he asked.

"I plan to stay for about one year," was my response.

"One year in Japan is not too long," the rector replied, "because there are so many things to be seen."

Then he asked, "Where will you go after leaving Japan?"

"I shall return to Europe, via China and India."

"I see. But for now, you will surely want to see a bit of California, am I right?" he asked.

"Oh, yes!" I answered, "that is my intention, as California is said to be one of the most beautiful places in all of North America!"

"Yes, that's what people say," answered the rector, smiling. "You can see for yourself if this is true!"

"I know my impression of California will be very positive," I replied. "The little bit I have seen up to now is so beautiful that it has already surpassed my expectations!"

Rector Harold Ring smiled at my fascination. I explained: "This morning was the first time I have seen California, so it is admittedly only a first impression. But this one little glimpse is sufficient to convince me of the beauty of your entire state."

"What is it that have you seen?" asked the Rector, curiously.

"I am amazed," I replied. "that, although I came in wintertime, just before Christmas, I am surrounded by an incredible wealth of beauty. There are abundant flowers. The lawns are green and velvety smooth, and the trees are in splendid bloom, the likes of which can only be seen in spring or early summer elsewhere. This magnificent nature – in the middle of winter! – is what delights me!"

"I am glad," said the friendly principal, "that our winter landscape is so pleasing to you. We are so used to it that we do not find it extraordinary!"

"Do you have any winter here at all?" I asked.

"Yes, we have. But our winter is what you see now."

"Does one ever see snow and ice here?" I asked.

"Snow and ice?" exclaimed the rector. "Oh, no, never. Most people here have never seen snow in their lives! Snow falls about once every fifty years. Ice sports, like skating, are completely unknown here."

"What a paradise!" I cried. "Always sunny, warm, blooming and fertile!"

"That is our wealth," said the principal.

"I have heard," I continued, "that California provides half of the world with wine and tropical fruits, so to speak."

"Well," said the modest principal, "we do grow fruit plentifully here."

"And on top of such abundance is the sheer beauty of the countryside!" I added. "It seems that California is not only one of the most fertile, but also one of the most beautiful places in the whole world."

"Perhaps that is so," replied the Rector, thoughtfully. "During your stay with us, you will have ample opportunity to have a look at both countryside and cities in California. I would suggest you take the train along the Pacific coast, for example, to the south. There you will see the beautiful and rapidly emerging city of Los Angeles, and on the way there, the beautiful little town of Santa Barbara. The stretch from here to Los Angeles can be done by train in one day, easily. In Los Angeles, you can also see the world-famous Hollywood section, where many films are made."

I thanked the generous and friendly Rector, resolving to make that trip at my best opportunity. But, for now, I did not wish to disturb my busy landlord any longer. The principal pushed a buzzer, and soon afterwards I heard steps approaching. The door opened and a young gentleman entered the room.

"Will you please accompany our guest to his rooms?" said the Rector to this man. And so, I was shown to my rooms. This young gentleman was one of the university professors. He assisted me with the utmost friendliness, guiding me to my room and reviewing with me the house rules. As he lived nearby, he promised to look after me during the first few days of my stay.

"Should you need anything," he said as he shook my hand to say goodbye, "please knock on my door. I am close by, after all."

"Thank you very much for your kindness," I said.

Instead of answering, he squeezed my hand again, and rushed off to his room.

NONNI IN AMERICA

CHAPTER 53

THE AMIABLE CALIFORNIANS

When I was all by myself in my sitting-room, I had the chance to finally relax a bit. I made myself comfortable in an armchair and pondered my new setting.

It sank in that I had managed to cross the vast North American continent in its entirety from East to West, and thus I finally reached the shores of the huge Pacific Ocean, the so-called "Still Sea." I was now in one of the most beautiful states in America, one of the most splendid regions of the whole world, this most delightful California. Only the mighty "Still Sea" separated me from the actual destination of my world trip, namely, the vast mysterious Asian countries: Japan, China, India. Even just being here in California felt as though I was as far away as I could be from where anyone could find me.

I was startled, then, when someone found me immediately! While I was sitting and resting, a knock came to my door.

The door opened, and a young gentleman entered my room. I got up quickly to greet him.

"Good morning, Sir!" he said, in a friendly way. "May I disturb you for a moment?"

I assured him: "You do not disturb me at all. Please, have a seat." I pointed to a chair next to the table.

The friendly visitor sat down and said: "I heard that you have come here from Europe, and that you are going to stay for a while in order to get to know California a bit."

"Yes, you are right," I answered. "I have come from Europe, and I have already spent a few months in the United States and Canada. I am eager to visit California, now, with special interest, because California is known as a wonderland throughout the world."

The young man smiled at me and said: "You must be planning to stay here for a few weeks, maybe even a few months, in order to get to know California and its people thoroughly."

"Yes, that is my plan," I replied.

"And, then, where will you go?" asked the young man.

This question gave me the chance to find out if I had accurately estimated the breadth of the Pacific Ocean. "I have planned to travel from here across the Pacific Ocean to Japan," I said.

His response assured me: "Going from here to Japan across the immensely wide Pacific will be a mighty long voyage!"

"Yes, but that is exactly what makes this trip so interesting for me!" I answered. "My first leg of the journey, from Europe to America – across the Atlantic Ocean – took five days and five nights on a fast European giant steamship. I am guessing that will be short compared to my next leg, from here to Japan."

"Yes, you are right. The voyage from here to Japan is much longer than crossing the Atlantic Ocean from Europe to America, and even continuing on to California."

"Then, the American continent from New York to California is as broad as the Atlantic Ocean between Europe and America?" I asked, surprised.

"Yes!" was his response. "The width of the United States from New York to San Francisco is almost the same as the width of the Atlantic Ocean between Europe and the United States."

I learned that this friendly young gentleman had become a Californian after moving from southern Germany. He chatted with me for a while longer, and then he offered me his services if I might need them at any time. After that, he wished me all the best during my stay in California.

Once more alone in my room, I abandoned myself to my thoughts. I was amazed by the friendliness of those who did not know me at all —

everybody was eager to serve and help me. The amiability of these Californians was as pleasant as their delightfully sunny climate.

Lukewarm air breezed through the window towards me. The sky was covered with light clouds. A thermometer hung outside, in front of the window. I had a look: 59 degrees Fahrenheit...15 degrees Celsius, on the 24th of December, in winter!

I heard steps approaching once again, and shortly afterwards, another knock on my door.

"Come in!" I shouted again.

The door opened to a new visitor, whom I was surprised to hear speak German. I expected to hear only English spoken in California!

"Good day!" I said, extending my hand in greeting. "Is it possible you are German?"

"Yes, I am German!" he replied. "And, since I know you speak my mother tongue, I wanted to stop in and wish you a good day!"

"That was very kind of you," I said. "May I ask you for your name?"

"My name is easy to remember," he replied. "In a nutshell: my name is Stern."

"I am very pleased to meet you. You must surely feel happy to live in such a paradise."

"Certainly I do!" he said. "But nevertheless, I long for Germany."

I answered: "I can understand that very well. That happens to all of us. Our fatherland always attracts us. What keeps you here?"

"I don't live at this university," he replied, "but I am employed in the city, in the Municipal Hospital. Some time ago, I heard that you would be coming here from New York, and I resolved to invite you for a visit. We would be pleased if you could give a lecture!"

Quite honored, I said, "I accept your invitation with great pleasure. But who shall be my audience? Not the patients?"

"No, not the patients, but the nurses. The hospital is very big, you know. It holds several thousand beds. It is the biggest hospital in San Francisco. Your audience will be several hundred nurses."

"I would be honored," I answered. "Hopefully, the nurses will be able to share some of my stories with their patients."

The date of my lecture at this big Municipal Hospital was decided, and my visitor promised to pick me up. Mr. Stern took leave with a friendly departure: "See you soon! I shall return here to take you there myself."

CHAPTER 54

SAN FRANCISCO MUNICIPAL HOSPITAL

On the day of the lecture, I was taken by Mr. Stern in a car from the university to the Municipal Hospital of San Francisco. Our route took us over a good number of the charming metropolitan hills, up and down. We finally reached the immense hospital. We got out in front of the main entrance, and my friend guided me into the building. It was just before noon.

We found the coatroom past some wide corridors, and then we entered a vast hall. I stopped to look around this room for a few moments.

"This is the main dining hall of the Municipal Hospital," Mr. Stern told me.

Uncountable small tables, each with shining white tablecloth, filled the spacious hall. Around each table were several chairs.

Mr. Stern led me to one of the tables. From there we had an unhindered view of the whole hall. After sitting down, Mr. Stern said to me: "These tables will all fill up quickly, because in a few minutes it will be time for lunch."

I asked: "Who will be dining here?"

"The doctors," he answered. "This hall is reserved exclusively for doctors exclusively, as well as foreign guests."

No sooner had he said this than a door opened and two gentlemen in medical garb entered. They were engrossed in conversation. They did not notice us, but sat down at one of the tables and continued their conversation there.

Shortly afterwards, many more gentlemen, both elderly and young, came into the hall. Most of them were also engaged in conversation. They spread out in groups across the vast hall, sitting two, three or four at a time. No sooner had they taken their seats there than many waiters in white uniforms came into the hall. They distributed dishes and drinks to the gentlemen at every table.

NONNI IN AMERICA

"These are all doctors in this big hospital," said my friend once again. Then, he added with a smile: "You have probably not very often dined with so many healers in your life!"

"You are right!" I replied. "This is truly the first time in my life that I have had such an honor!"

After a short pause I asked my friend: "The care in this big hospital must be especially good, I am guessing?"

"Yes, without exaggeration. Care in this big hospital is excellent."

"In that case, it must also be rather expensive, yes?"

"Expensive?" repeated Mr. Stern, "Oh, no. On the contrary, it is unusually affordable. Even cheap!"

I looked at Mr. Stern in amazement, and asked: "How so? In such a great hospital where everything is first class, how could the care here cost so little? Every patient here must pay at least five to six dollars a day."

"Five to six dollars a day…" repeated Mr. Stern. "Patient care is probably worth that amount. However, you would not pay that much."

"Then, let's say four dollars?"

"It's not four dollars a day, either."

"Three dollars?"

"That is also still too high."

I looked at my friend with astonishment and said: "Three dollars a day in such a hospital is too much? I cannot comprehend that!"

"I can very well understand your astonishment," said Mr. Stern, "but you are assuming one has to pay for the care they receive. But that is not the case: The patients here get everything for free."

Completely astounded, I asked: "From where does the money come from then?"

"I shall tell you now," replied Mr. Stern. "Not everyone has the right to get free care here. This great privilege is granted only to the inhabitants of the city of San Francisco. For those the city of San Francisco takes care and pays generously because this big hospital is the so-called Municipal Hospital of the City of San Francisco."

Now everything was clear to me, yet I was still surprised to think that a hospital of this kind, and of this size, and of this excellence, would grant such first class care free of charge to all inhabitants of the city.

CHAPTER 55

A LECTURE TO THE ANGELS

When we finished lunch, we went to another hall, in which my lecture for the nurses was to take place.

The lecture hall was very spacious, with several hundred chairs lined up there. On one end stood a lectern on a high platform, to which several steps led. When we arrived, the hall was still completely empty.

While we stood waiting, a strange noise came from somewhere above in the building. It sounded like footsteps from many people moving about in one of the upper floors. Puzzled, I looked at Mr. Stern.

"Those are your listeners, who are coming now," he said.

The footsteps became more and more distinct and came closer and closer.

"Will my audience be nurses only, or will there be other people, too?" I asked.

"There will only be nurses attending," replied Mr. Stern, "but not every nurse of this hospital, by far; only as many as can be seated. This hall is not big enough to hold all the nurses at once."

The sound grew nearer and nearer. Finally, the doors opened, and a whole wave of young girls in snow white clothes streamed into the vast auditorium.

I ascended to the lectern and waited till the hall was completely filled. Then I gave a signal with a small bell nearby. Everybody sat down… and the lecture began. I noticed how greatly the lighting in the hall had changed. What gave the effect of sunshine was the room light reflecting off so many dazzling white uniforms in the audience! I talked to them for a good hour, as usual, describing several of my adventures in Europe. When time was up, the attentive young nurses thanked me by applauding energetically. Then they got up and made to go back to their patients.

But then, I got a rare surprise: While the nurses were leaving the hall, four of them stayed behind at the exit. All four approached the lectern. As it seemed they wanted to say something to me, I remained and waited. One of them asked: "May we talk with you for a moment?"

"Yes, for sure," I replied, "it's my pleasure, you are all welcome."

Then she continued: "We would like to introduce ourselves to you," she said, "because we all are your compatriots, more or less."

I looked at them, amazed, and said: "Help me understand!"

"You will see in a moment," she continued. "We four come from the Scandinavian countries. You are an Icelander, and since Iceland belongs to the Scandinavian North, we all are compatriots!"

Then she took a piece of chalk and wrote her Danish name on the blackboard beside the lectern, saying: "I am a Dane."

Then it was the turn of the second girl. She introduced herself as a Swedish girl and wrote her Swedish name on the blackboard – just like the first one.

What a big surprise for me! There I was, suddenly caught up in a small, amiable, European-Nordic community!

But that was not all, because now came the biggest surprise! The third nurse also took a piece of chalk, went to the blackboard and said: "I am an Icelander!"

I must admit that I thought she must be joking. Meanwhile, the fourth nurse wrote her Norwegian name on the blackboard, next to the other three.

I read the four names over. They were all true Nordic names: one Danish, one Swedish, one Norwegian and – one Icelandic! It was not a joke! I was quite glad to meet these amiable Scandinavian women. We talked together for a little while. I learned that their families lived in San

Francisco and that there were several other Nordic families in California after all. A few days later, the father of the Icelandic nurse was pleased to visit with me. He said he had lived in California for many years, but still felt as an Icelander, to my surprise and delight.

CHAPTER 56

DEPARTURE FOR JAPAN

I remained in San Francisco for more than two months, and during all that time, I enjoyed the hospitality of Rector Harald Ring in his university.

However, at the beginning of March, it was time to leave California and go by the Japanese boat "Chichibu Maru" to Japan across the great "Still Sea," the Pacific Ocean. The "Chichibu Maru" was bound for Yokohama, a big port near Tokyo, the capital of Japan. That Japanese steamer was scheduled to leave America on March 4th, 1937.

I only needed a few days to prepare my departure. I used that short span of time to say goodbye to my friends and acquaintances in the city, and especially to thank my hosts for their hospitality.

On the last day, I went through the big building to say goodbye to my companions. When I stopped in on one of the professors, whom I knew quite well, he said to me: "As you are going directly to Japan, maybe you would like to shake hands with our three Japanese gentlemen here in the house, to say goodbye?"

"I will do that, with great pleasure," I answered. "Maybe they have requests for me to take back to their home."

"In that case," said the professor, "I will take you to them immediately."

I accepted his offer with thanks, and he led me to the three unknown men. As we walked, my guide said: "Perhaps you would like to hear about these people."

"Oh yes, I am very interested," I replied.

"You may be surprised," he said, "when I tell you that these men are our cooks. I have to add that all three men hold the highest respect of all of us in this house because of their noble integrity."

I listened with the greatest interest as he continued: "First, the head chef is Sumida Umeichi; he is fifty years old. The second is Nakamoto and the third is Yasuba. Mr. Umeichi has worked for us as head chef for twenty years.

Although he earns several weeks of vacation every year, he has never wanted to take time off, and he has worked all these years without any break. The other two have likewise seldom taken time off, each only for a short time. During all these years, we have had nothing but praise for these men."

My interest in these three marvelous men grew doubly great, and I went eagerly with my guide into the kitchen of this big institution.

The three Japanese men were in the midst of their culinary work. They received us very politely, but did not turn their attention away from their task. I greeted the head chef, a big, strong man, and said to him: "Today, I will be leaving California to go to Japan, your fatherland, on the 'Chichibu Maru'. If you wish me to take any greeting along, I will gladly do so."

"Thank you very much," replied the head chef, "but all my relatives and friends there are long dead. But – I know! You can say 'Hello' to Japan!"

I was touched by that short request, and I marveled at the emotion beneath his words. His two helpers also responded in a friendly way to all that I said, yet did so without getting distracted from their work for a single moment.

I asked them, "As the name of my ship will be the 'Chichibu Maru,' can you tell me what those words mean?"

"It is the name of one of our Imperial princes," answered the head chef.

The three men wished me a happy voyage and much pleasure during my stay in their fatherland. We parted with friendly handshakes. I left the kitchen feeling as if I had spoken with noble men of a higher class, so dignified were these three Japanese cooks of the kitchen in the American University of San Francisco.

Soon after my farewell tour of the whole building, I was taken by car to the ship. Thus, the Western world was about to lie behind me. And, with great expectations, I turned my eyes looking forward to the Far East.

www.ingramcontent.com/pod-product-compliance
Lightning Source LLC
Chambersburg PA
CBHW070255240426
43661CB00057B/2559